FIRETEAM™ Exam Review Guide

By Lewis Morris

FIRETEAM™ is a trademark of National Testing Network, Inc., which was not involved in the production of, and does not endorse or sponsor this product. This review manual was designed to provide accurate and authoritative information regarding the subject matter covered. It is sold with the understanding that the author and publisher are not engaged in offering legal, accounting, or other professional service. If legal advice or other expert assistance is required, the services of a competent professional should be sought.

Copyright © 2017 Network4Learning, Inc.

All rights reserved.

ISBN-13: 978-1517478070

ISBN-10: 1517478073

DEDICATION

This Exam Review Guide is dedicated to George Gordon

CONTENTS

	Acknowledgments	I
1	About the Exam	3
2	Test Preparation Strategies	5
3	How to Beat Testing Anxiety	21
4	Exam Subareas and Practice Questions	33
5	Reading Comprehension	34
6	Number Facility	129
9	Mathematical Reasoning	134
10	Human Relations	140
11	Mechanical Ability	185
12	Glossary	221

ACKNOWLEDGMENT

I would like to acknowledge the hard work and talent of Gabriella who assisted with the editing and cover art for this edition.

About the Exam

Human Relations

Part I

Part I of the Video Human Relations Test focuses on teamwork and human relations skills and is presented in a firefighting context. Candidates watch a video segment, then choose the BEST course of action in a multiple-choice format. Once they have chosen the BEST possible course of action, they are asked to identify the WORST possible course of action. This test is presented on a computer, and the items play without stopping.

Part II

In addition to answering the Part I questions on the Video-Based Human Relations Test, candidates are instructed to observe the behaviors of the individual firefighters portrayed. They can observe behavior on multiple occasions for many of the firefighters. Part II of the Video-Based Human Relations Test consists of questions about these firefighters and their behaviors. Part II immediately follows Part I.

Mechanical Abilities Test

The Mechanical Abilities Test is a multiple-choice test presented on video. Candidates see detailed introductions to animated machinery, then are asked questions about the machinery. Most of the questions are about basic mechanical objects such as valves and simple tools. They are also asked to answer troubleshooting type questions and observe system operations for problems. All the questions can be answered based on common sense and observation of how everyday objects work.

Reading Comprehension Test

This test is based on training material, and candidates are required to choose a word that best completes a sentence. This section may also test basic reasoning skills within a reading context such as deductive and inductive reasoning.

Math Test

This math test is presented within the context of firefighting. The questions are video based. Candidates must complete the calculations in their heads. Areas tested include addition, subtraction, multiplication, division and proportions. No scrap paper or calculators are allowed. All calculations are to be done in your head.

The test is approximately 2 ½ hours long.

Test Preparation Strategies:
Beginning Your Preparation

Begin preparing and studying as soon as possible. You want to engage your long-term memory, which can only be done over a period of months.

1. Find a regular time in your schedule when you can devote a half an hour or more of quiet study time.

2. Set a schedule and stick to it. Discuss your schedule with your family, so that everybody understands your need for uninterrupted study time.

3. Start practicing your memory skills in everyday life. If you are walking and see a billboard, take 10 seconds to look at it carefully. Then, as you go about your way, try to remember details such as color, names, and dates. If you take public transportation, there are numerous opportunities to practice this method, because you have a multitude of different advertisements to view.

4. Study without distractions to the best of your ability. Turn off your phone. Inform people close to you that you will be unavailable during that period, so that there is no expectation of a returned phone call.

5. Be sure you are getting enough sleep because proper rest will greatly affect your concentration and memory skills. Create a peaceful sleep environment by eliminating lights and sounds, obtaining quality pillows, and limiting nighttime activities. Do not eat within an hour of bed, and avoid caffeine and chocolate a few hours before sleep.

6. Limiting or stopping alcohol consumption will assist you in the firefighter vetting process. Alcohol can seriously affect your memory and ability to concentrate in several specific ways. Being intoxicated has been proven to negatively affect abstract thinking skills in people for at least six weeks. Alcohol affects sleep by contributing to sleep apnea, and many people who drink only moderately have been shown to sleep poorly. Regular use of alcohol contributes to weight gain and raises blood pressure.

7. Motivate yourself. Find a way to be enthusiastic in your preparation. Prove to yourself that you can earn a high score and make the grade. Keep a positive outlook and make it a constructive experience.

8. Start early. Begin preparing as soon as the exam is announced.

9. Avoid last minute cramming. Cramming does not work well, but refreshing your memory the night before the exam does positively impact performance.

10. Without interruptions, give yourself enough time to complete each sub area in a single sitting. This will give you more confidence and provide you with a realistic expectation for the actual exam.

11. Develop careful reading habits. You must become an active reader. For example, rephrase each question in your words to make sure you understand the question. Re-check your answers, and make sure your choice correctly answers the question asked.

12. Don't try to memorize practice questions, instead focus on the process of critically reading and analyzing each question.

13. Concentrate on the sections of the exam you find most challenging.

14. Budget your time accordingly to practice more difficult areas.

    o Focus on completing one sub-area question set at a time. Go through your wrong answers and locate the correct answer by reading through the review material. Complete an error analysis early in your studying so that you work through any deficiencies early enough to gain confidence in the material.

    o Create a set of flashcards by taking any unfamiliar words from the glossary and putting them on index cards. Write out the definition on the reverse side of the card.

The Night Before the Exam

Briefly, review the practice questions you have already completed. Focus on your successful responses. Your goal is to refresh your memory and reduce anxiety. Set two alarm clocks and leave an hour before going to bed. Refrain from looking at a computer screen for at least an hour before bed, because light emitted from the screen has been shown in studies to contribute to sleeplessness.

Getting Ready the Day of the Examination

1. Stick to your normal routine as much as possible. Some suggestions may not be in your normal routine, but they usually allow most people to perform their best.

2. Get adequate sleep. Most adults perform best with 7-8 hours of sleep. Adopt this pattern at least a week before the exam. Even if you have trouble sleeping the night before the exam; don't worry. If you have rested well for several days leading up to the exam, your body will adjust, and your performance will remain elevated.

3. Get up early enough to have a light, balanced breakfast. Set your alarm, and have a backup alarm set as well.

4. Minimize the use of outside influences (food, caffeine, nicotine, entertainment) that might over or under stimulate you. Primarily, do not do anything too radical - and not too different than what is normal for you.

5. Leave for the test early enough to allow for the traffic, weather, and parking. Resolve childcare needs well in advance. Give yourself ample time to settle in at the test site.
On the morning of the exam, log into a local traffic site, and

consider using a traffic app such as "Waze" to keep updated on traffic issues. If possible, have somebody drive you to the test, or take public transportation. Imagine how stressful it would be if you ran into traffic and then had to struggle to find parking.

6. Eat before the test. Having food in your stomach will give you energy and help you focus; however, avoid heavy foods which can make you groggy.

At the Exam Site

1. Listen to instructions from hall monitors and test proctors. If you are unsure of any aspect of the test, make sure that you understand the instructions and ask questions at the designated time before the test begins.

2. Use your time carefully. Do not rush. You should have enough time to cover the entire test if you move through it steadily. Do not spend too much time on any one question. Read questions slowly enough to make sure you understand, but don't spend too much time on any one question.

3. Read each question and all the answers carefully. Do not jump to an answer before you have completely read all the alternatives.

4. Respond to each question separately. The answer to one question is not meant to lead you to an answer on a subsequent question.

5. Answer all the questions. Use your informed judgment to make a choice between alternate answers. Although this may feel like an you are making an "educated guess", you are

demonstrating a degree of knowledge - not just blindly guessing.

6. Don't worry about trick questions. None of the questions in this test is designed to trick the test-taker. The test is intended to allow you to demonstrate your understanding of the assessed material. Avoid reading too much into a question.

Go to the bathroom before walking into the exam room. You don't want to waste any time worrying about your bodily needs during the test.

Immediately after the Exam

As soon as you finish, find a quiet space to sit down and record your thoughts and about the exam. Write down as many specific things as you can. This will help you, should you desire to take a test for a similar municipal job title. This firefighter exam is very similar in format and content to other civil service exams offered in throughout the country. Recording your thoughts will assist you in developing an even better study plan for future exams.

Preparing for the Examination

Tests are given to assure selection of the most qualified persons into fire departments while providing all candidates a chance to compete fairly. The department will use several kinds of tests and screening methods to gauge your readiness to enter their employment. The written exam is only the first component of the overall selection process. Knowing the rationale for this test and having a realistic perception of the job requirements can improve your chance to demonstrate those qualities most desirable in professional firefighter.

This test is designed to assess:

- Problem solving (i.e. reasoning and the application of rules)

- Writing skills

- Reading comprehension

- Personality characteristics

In the days and weeks before the exam, these suggestions are offered:

1. Complete the practice exam offered on the nationaltestingnetwork.com website. Schedule to take the entry level law enforcement exam offered by the National Testing Network, as it is a very similar format to the firefighter exam and is delivered in the same format.

2. Make sure that you accurately complete all forms and requirements prior to the exam.

3. Take some time every day to improve your reading and writing skills. These skills are important for effective performance since firefighter recruits and will be assessed by the test. Of course, these skills are also important in many other lines of work, including promotions within the fire department.

4. Practice taking other tests. Check with local civil service commissions for upcoming exams, and consider taking the law enforcement officer exam offered by the National Testing

Network, as it is produced by the same folks who produce the firefighter exam you are planning to take.

6. The more confident you are in your abilities, the better you will do on the exam. The way to become confident is to practice as many questions before the exam as possible. There is a very strong correlation between the number of practice questions completed and the individual's ability to perform well on the exam.

7. Strive to stay focused. Practice regaining focus when you feel your mind wandering. Successful test-takers are aware of when their mind wanders and have strategies for regaining focus. It is also normal for negative, self-defeating thoughts to enter your mind after a series of difficult questions. Recognize this, and use a strategy for eliminating negativity. One way is to create a positive image of relaxing on the couch and watching a favorite movie after the exam. Think to yourself "I am almost there. Let's get back in the game and do this. Then, I can go home and relax". Positive self-talk is very powerful.

Maintain a positive attitude. This exam is an opportunity for you to show your skills and abilities, and a positive attitude can have an influential impact on increasing your test score. There are a few ways to fine-tune your attitude toward taking this exam:

- Look at this exam as a challenge but try not to get overly stressed by thinking about it too much.

- Remember that passing this exam is the first step in the selection process for entrance to the fire academy, but it is not the only piece of information used to make that decision.

Understand the Test Format and Requirements

1. Read all the directions carefully.

2. Know how to correctly use the computer terminal. Ask for clarification if you do not understand how the examination is administered.

3. Know that you have two hours and thirty minutes to complete the examination. You are responsible for budgeting the allotted time. Bring a watch and monitor it.

Understand the test questions:

1. Read each question carefully. Try to answer the question before you look at the choices. If you know the answer, compare it to the available choices and pick the choice closest in meaning to your answer.

2. Recognize and make note of *qualifiers*. *Qualifiers* are words that change a statement including: always, most, equal, good, and bad. In a multiple-choice question, qualifiers can make an answer on a test question the correct option or an incorrect answer. For example, the following two statements are nearly identical: It *often* rains in Los Alamos. It is *always* raining in Los Alamos. The first statement is true, while the word "always" in the second statement makes it false. Be aware of qualifiers that appear in test questions or in the answer selection.

To tackle qualifiers, you need to know the qualifier groups:
- All, most, some, none (no)
- Always, usually, sometimes, never
- Great, much, little, no
- More than, equal to, or less than
- Good, bad
- Is, is not

Whenever one qualifier from a group is used in an answer choice, substitute each of the others from the group. Then, you can tell which of the qualifiers fits best. If the best qualifier is the one in the answer selection, then the choice is correct. If the best qualifier is another one from the family, then the answer choice is false.

3. Negatives are words like no, not, none and never, and they are frequently in prefixes like il-, as in illogical, un-, as in uninterested, or im- as in impatient. Recognize negatives because they reverse the meaning of a sentence. For example, the prefix in- causes this statement to be false:

"Because he based his research on ***incorrect*** data, his argument was imperfect."

Proceed through the questions strategically:

1. Do not get stuck on words or sentences you do not understand. You may still get the main idea of a sentence or paragraph without understanding an individual word or the meaning of a sentence.

2. Use the *process of elimination.* If you do not know the answer to a question, first eliminate those choices that are clearly incorrect. Then, put a mark next to each remaining choice to indicate its likelihood (e.g., maybe, likely, or probable). This will save you time, particularly if you decide to skip the question and come back to it later, by reducing the number of answers you must reread and re-evaluate before making your final choice.

3. Guess. There is no penalty for selecting an incorrect answer in this examination, so answer every question. If the examination period is about to end and you will not be able to complete all the questions, reserve three to five minutes toward the very end of the section to answer these questions. While guesses throughout the final responses may not be

correct, the alternative is to leave these questions blank and receive no credit.

4. In "All of the above" and "None of the above" choices, if you are certain one of the statements is true don't choose "None of the above" **or** one of the statements are false don't choose "All of the above". In a question with an "All of the above" choice, if you see at least two correct statements, then "All of the above" is probably the answer.

How to Avoid Making Errors

Each one of us has strengths and weaknesses concerning tests. This section will give you tools to identify weaknesses in your test-taking ability. The process of comparing your responses with the answer key and identifying patterns will help you tackle recurring problems with your testing skills.

The sample questions contained within each section in this guide are very similar to the kinds of questions that will appear on the actual examination. Focus on the questions you got wrong. Read through the test-taking strategies below to help you avoid making the same mistakes in the future.

There are several possible reasons for choosing an incorrect answer. Seven common reasons, along with suggestions to minimize repeating such errors, are presented below.

Why We Make Incorrect Responses

1. <u>Answer Omissions:</u>

It is very easy to skip a question by hitting the "Next" button twice. Be mindful of the number of questions to ensure that you leave no questions blank.

You may also miss questions because you failed to provide an answer or were forced to quickly select any answer (guess) before time was called. If either of these situations happened, consider the underlying error.

Possible reasons include:

    a. You may have missed a question because you skipped it then failed to return to it later.

    b. You may have lost track of the time before the examination period was about to end, and this occurred before you could mark any remaining unanswered questions. Check your watch frequently, so that you can monitor the amount of time you have left.

    c. You may have been forced to make guesses for questions placed toward the end of the examination. Rather than skipping questions and returning later, you possibly devoted too much time working on difficult questions earlier in the exam. Skipping questions that are hard may give you more time with later questions; and therefore, you may have a better chance of answering them correctly.

    d. You may have skipped difficult questions, but in returning to them did not save yourself time by reducing the number of answer choices (e.g., maybe, likely, or probable).

2. <u>Misreading a question or answer by overlooking a key word:</u>

Because the exam is on a computer screen, you will not be able to underline key terms and phrases. Use your finger to underline a key term or phrase. It will not be visible on the screen, but the physical act of tracing an imaginary line under the term or phrase will make it stand out in your mind.

3. <u>Not knowing the meaning of one or more key terms:</u>

When you don't know a definition, reread the sentence to decode its meaning. Try to understand the main idea of the sentence or paragraph. The exact definition of the word should become clear once you understand the general context of the sentence around it. Study the glossary; it will give you a solid working background of fire department terminology.

4. <u>Difficulty distinguishing between important vs. inconsequential parts of a question:</u>

Typically, these are the questions you should skip until the end of the test. Break up the question into smaller parts; then, concentrate on one part at a time. Returning to the difficult questions, read the possible answers before reading the questions. This helps direct concentration while reading the question. Also, identify the topic sentences that are usually the first and last sentences in a question. Read difficult questions twice.

It is typically a best practice to read for the first time for the main idea. Do not waste time on challenging words or phrases you do not understand. Search for context clues the second time, reading for more detailed understanding. The first reading will provide an overview, enabling the second reading to facilitate a more detailed analysis. Finally, visualize the content by drawing a mental picture.

5. Not knowing how to combine different types of information:

These questions require rearranging information in the correct logical sequence. On the screen, use your finger to underline important pieces of information. And then, compare this information with the possible answers point-by-point. Concentrate on eliminating the wrong answers first.

6. Choosing an answer simply because it "looks" good:

Several factors may cause you to choose incorrect answers that appear to "look good":

   a. An incorrect answer may contain exact wording from the original question.

   b. An incorrect answer may contain a phrase or sentence from the original question presented in a different way. For example, a fact that is negated in the question may be presented as a positive in an answer choice.

   c. An incorrect answer may overstate what the question has detailed using deceptive qualifiers. For example, if the question states, "Some fires...," the incorrect answer may state, "All fires ...."

Some strategies for avoiding incorrect answers that "look good" include:

   a. Formulate your own answer before you review the answer choices. This will make you less likely to choose an answer that just "looks good."

   b. Rate the likelihood of each probable answer before choosing. Think in terms of "That's it!", "Probable", "Not Likely", "No Way!".

c. Beware of choosing answers based on unverified assumptions. In this sense, your experience can work against you. Answer only based on the material presented in the test question.

d. Stick strictly to the facts described in the test question. Carefully watch out for words such as "only," "never," "always," "whenever," and "all". If you see one of these terms, take a few seconds to check that you understand the implications of the vocabulary in the question.

e. Beware of answers containing exact words or phrases from the question material. Do not assume that such answers are correct.

f. In your inner dialogue, prepare a defense for your answer choice. Find something in the test question that will allow you to give a strong defense for your answer. How would you explain your answer to another person?

7. You may not know why you missed a question. If you do not understand why you missed a question, we suggest you review the preparation guide again. Also, talk with someone else who may be taking the test to compare preparation strategies.

SUMMARY:

- Read the question before you look at the answer.

- Come up with your response before looking at the possible answers; this way, the choices given on the test won't trick you.

- Eliminate answers you know aren't right.

- Read all the choices before choosing your answer.

- There is no guessing penalty, so always take an educated guess and select an answer.

- Don't keep changing your answer. Unless you misread the question, usually, your first choice is the right one.

How to Beat Testing Anxiety

What is testing anxiety?

Test anxiety is nervousness that arises from high-stakes testing assessment. Our bodies react with chemical and physical changes in response to stress. In a sense, testing anxiety is our body's way of telling us that something important is about to happen. Because of this heightened state of readiness, we feel the pressure of the upcoming exam in many ways that can cause unease and discomfort. At times, these feelings may become overwhelming and negatively affect the test-taker's performance.

What causes testing anxiety?

The pressure to get a good grade, the high-stakes nature of an exam, the perceived difficulty of the exam, and the cost of the exam all contribute to the feelings of test anxiety.

What are the physical symptoms of testing anxiety?

- sweating palms and forehead
- sore neck and back from tense muscles
- headache
- nausea
- increased heart rate
- difficulty sleeping

What are the mental symptoms of testing anxiety?

- anger
- frustration or "being short" with family, friends, and coworkers
- mental blocking (drawing a "blank" on questions)
- looping negative thoughts
- impaired ability to focus
- feeling sleepy and yawning during the exam

- doing poorly on an exam, even though you were confident in the material
- having difficulty remembering the definitions of key terms
- ambient thoughts during the exam

How can I reduce testing anxiety?

- Practice. With enough practice answering similar questions, you will become desensitized to some of the anxiety producing stimuli.
- Learn the material over a long period vs. attempting to "cram" for the exam. By studying material over a month or more, you will engage your long-term memory. This type of memory is less affected by testing anxiety.
- Duplicate the testing environment as closely as possible and practice in that environment.
- Visit the testing site if possible.
- Take similar exams prior to taking this test. (For example, take an upcoming corrections officer exam a month or two before the firefighter exam. This will boost your confidence and desensitize you to pre-test anxiety. It will also familiarize you with testing policies and increase your cognitive stamina).
- Learn to focus on the material by concentrating on important terms from the glossary and practice questions.
- Create a detailed study plan and schedule.
- Organize your study materials to eliminate frustration.
- Utilize relaxation techniques such as stretching, breathing, posture, and walking.

How can controlling the study environment help manage testing anxiety?

- Set up your study environment so that it is conducive to learning and reduces stress. Find an area that has no interruptions or noise.
- Set up lighting so that there are no shadows or excessive brightness that cause squinting or the straining of eye

muscles. If possible, add an incandescent cool white bulb to the lighting to help balance the colors.
- Control the temperature, so you are comfortable but alert.
- Choose a chair that is not so comfortable that it causes drowsiness and has a straight back to enhance postural breathing.
- Do not study in bed. Your brain is conditioned to sleep in bed, and your sessions will not be as productive. Your sleep may also be disturbed by studying immediately prior to bed time.
- Have everything necessary to work close at hand.

How can I prepare for testing anxiety?

- Recognize it as a serious part of test preparation
- Develop a study plan and stick to it
- Study long-term, over a period of a month or more
- Stay positive
- Resist feeling overwhelmed
- Learn an effective strategy for actively chasing away negative thoughts. Develop ways to recognize negative thoughts and have a specific strategy to confront them.
- Don't worry. Worrying is a waste of time and energy. As soon as you begin to feel worried, grab a book and do a few easy practice questions to move forward and boost confidence.

How do I confront testing anxiety when it occurs during the test?

- Stay engaged during the exam. Force your mind to refocus.
- Slow down. Anxiety changes our perception of time and tends to cause rushing.
- Breathe. Practice sitting straight with good posture and breathe deeply and slowly. If necessary, purse your lips while exhaling to reduce your breathing rate.
- Feeling tense can be helpful. Recognize that it is your body gearing up to do its best.
- Stay in control.

- Remember... the exam will pass quickly enough. Your job is to slow things down and stay in the game as long as possible.

How can I use positive self-talk to manage testing anxiety?

After the exam, write down your feelings. Focus on the positive elements of the experience. This will most likely not be the last test you take in your life, and creating a positive image in your mind will help you minimize test anxiety in the future. Focus on positive self-statements such as "I Did It!", "It wasn't that bad", "Studying really helped.", "Some of the questions were challenging, but I rose to the occasion.", and "The test was like a puzzle to solve".

How can goal-setting help me manage testing anxiety?

- Keep your goals realistic for studying. It is easy to be too optimistic about how much time you can devote to studying. When you can't study as much as you planned, it is then easy to become discouraged.
- Be sure your goals are your own. Don't allow friends and family to pressure you into something you don't really want to do. If you do become a member of the fire department, it will be you running into the burning building.
- Try not to juggle too many goals at one time. If you want to prepare for an important exam, try putting off other major commitments until the exam has passed.
- Write your goals down. Be specific. Describe in detail what you want to accomplish and what you are willing to do to earn this achievement. Try to keep a journal. In the journal, log your experiences and time studying. Record your thoughts and "A-ha! moments" as you learn along the way.
- Your goals should all have a definite expiration date.
- All goals should be specific and measurable. There should be an exact, concrete outcome in mind. For example, a goal might be: "I will earn a score of at least 98% on the

firefighter exam on (insert exam date)". This goal has a specific, measurable outcome with a clear timeline.

How can effective time-management help us eliminate testing anxiety?

- Begin by charting and calculating where your time goes every day. Chart what you do for a week. Look for dead spaces in time. Do you watch TV for a few hours a day? How much time do you spend on Facebook? Perhaps you like to watch a lot of sports. Find out how much time you spend sleeping and getting ready. Investigate if there are people in your life who unduly occupy your time. Once you have identified areas of your day that are not used efficiently, look for ways to limit the time lost. After careful evaluation, you will be amazed at how much free time you have to study in your schedule.
- Buy a day planner and chart out all your responsibilities. Carry this with you everywhere. Complete it in pencil, and do not feel bad if you must adjust it. Even if you find yourself wasting time; record it. The purpose is not to deny yourself free time for relaxation. Notwithstanding, look for areas of time you currently waste, and fill it with more productive time spent studying.
- Keep an eye out for procrastination. It is easy to get lazy and forestall responsibilities. The way to manage this is to start with an easy, short question set. Do a few practice questions in small increments; and then, go back to the previous activity. You will find, that after a while, it will become easy to motivate yourself once you know how to start.
- Learn how to say "NO" to friends, family, and coworkers. "Time-burglars" are everywhere. Look out for them and keep them at bay. Learn how to return calls when no one will answer, so you can leave a voicemail that says "sorry I didn't call you sooner, I was studying......". Tell people what you are doing and promise to be around after the test.
- Put your phone on silent for the time you are studying.

- Schedule ahead. Prepare a list of important events and plan to study around them.
- Map time backwards from the test date in your planning. First, black out any important dates such as holidays or family events. Then plan for short study and practice sessions. If possible, plan back a month or more.
- Also, plan specific time to practice relaxation and fitness. Schedule regular stretching, yoga, or walking.
- Plan your meals carefully. This is not the time to start a drastic weight-loss program. Instead plan regular, nutritious meals that will support your learning and memory. Foods high in energy and healthy fats should be included, while foods high in processed sugar should be avoided.
- By planning your time wisely, you may find that studying allocates more free time by wasting less time.

How to manage the effects of obsessing over the exam?

Some test-takers have the tendency to obsess over exams. This obsession could be a strong motivator to study; but oftentimes, it becomes paralyzing. If this speaks to you, learning to moderate your feelings is necessary to realize your goals. By scheduling thoughtful blocks of time for studying, then learning how to clear your mind, you will have a better chance of overcoming testing stress. When setting a goal, define the result you hope to achieve and the time and material resources you are willing to invest in achieving that goal. Once set, stick to the plan and seek satisfaction in your effort.

How do we overcome procrastination?

Most people procrastinate. Very few people can self-motivated consistently. For some people, however, procrastination is paralyzing and persistent. There are several reasons for procrastination:

- <u>Time management</u>: Many people just can't seem to balance their schedule to allot consistent time for studying. By the

time they sit down to study they are exhausted, or they are too overwhelmed to concentrate.
- <u>Negative beliefs or emotions</u>: Perhaps you performed poorly on another exam recently. Fear of failure drives you to delay working.
- <u>Feeling overwhelmed</u>: The exam seems insurmountably large and complex.
- <u>Personal problems</u>: Marriage, health, job situation, and finances… these issues creep in and take the candidate "off task".
- <u>Difficulty concentrating</u>: This issue can have many causes including diet, sleep, and outside stress. Learning how to control the physical environment is key to overcoming this issue.
- <u>Boredom</u>: Let's face it, studying is rarely thrilling. The way to overcome boredom is to start with short sessions and increase the study time as you go along.
- <u>Fear of failure</u>: Many people allow themselves to quit before they even start.

Why doesn't cramming work well?

Cramming is defined as studying intensely just prior to an exam. It generally includes an unfocused, disorganized, and often last-minute attempt to learn material typically covered over a long period. Cramming often results in sleep deprivation, exhausted eyes, and an overwhelmed short-term memory. Often, a test-taker will study the entire night before and arrive at the test site weary and unable to focus. Beyond the physical discomfort of cramming, there are very good reasons for spreading out study time from the perspective of brain function and memory. Successful test-takers know that the long-term memory is engaged during an exam. The only way to develop efficient long-term memory of subject matter is to study over a prolonged period.

What is the difference between short-term and long-term memory? Short-term memory is also called "working memory". It is used when doing something or performing a skill. Testing engages long-term memory and is best developed over a period of weeks or months.

When we cram, what information is remembered, and what is forgotten?

Cramming has been well-studied. Research demonstrates that while cramming, the first and last items are remembered, while the material studied during the middle of the session is forgotten. The speed at which a person reads is also significant. The slower the reading, the more material absorbed. Also, if the reader pauses regularly to mentally restate the content, the retention of information will improve.

What is the serial position effect?

The serial position effect is the tendency of a person to best recall the first and last items in a series but forget the middle. This effect is most apparent during cramming. When charted, the amount of retained material forms a reverse bell curve with the beginning and end containing the most content.

What is the primacy effect?

This is the tendency for the first items presented in a series to be remembered more easily than subsequent material. Those items at the beginning of a sequence are best imprinted in a person's memory. If you hear a long list of words, it is more likely that you will remember the words you heard first (at the beginning of the list) than words that occurred in the middle.

Why does reading slowly while cramming help?

Reading slowly while cramming can help you retain more information, because there is a cognitive echo; whereby, the brain repeats the material to itself. Therefore, reading slowly will help you process the material more extensively.

What are some tips for cramming?

- Study the most important information first and last. Study the least important information in the middle.
- Draw up a clear plan and break your studying up into segments.
- Focus on key terms and vocabulary.
- Read slowly. This will help your brain rehearse the information.

What about rumors?

Looking online at forums about the exam can be informative and helpful. Be careful, however, not to buy into the negativity that also exists online. I recommend not visiting them for a few weeks leading up to the exam. It is too easy to get "psyched out" and start second-guessing yourself.

Can I "beat" a test?

Simply put, no. The exam is professionally made and extensively field tested. The only way to beat the test is to practice numerous similar questions and, if possible, take similar exams (i.e. law enforcement/civil service). Practice and experience are key.

How do I overcome negative thoughts?

When under stress, it is completely natural to experience negative thoughts. The key to overcoming these thoughts is to first recognize them when they occur. And second, have a specific visualization to focus on when negative thoughts arise. For example, if you hit a hard string of questions, you might begin thinking that you are going to fail. Try to imagine yourself back at home in a few hours, eating your favorite take-out food and watching a movie.

Visualization is an effective method for reducing anxiety, especially when combined with physical relaxation techniques such as deep breathing, stretching, or yoga. The more specific and focused your imagery is, the more effective it will be.

What about yoga, deep breathing, posture, and walking?

Relaxation strategies can be very effective at relieving testing anxiety. Learning how to breathe properly and keeping good posture during the exam will increase your energy levels. If you are studying and begin to feel stressed, learn several slow stretches that help your posture and keep your back muscles supple. Yoga can be very beneficial, but you don't have to go out and join a studio. Start simple and incorporate balance into your routine.

Testing Anxiety Assessment Tool

Read through the responses below and assign a 0, 1, or 2 indicating the degree to which each statement reflects your feelings, 0 being none and 2 being great. Keep in mind that questions 1-10 are physical indicators and questions 11-20 are behavioral indicators.

1. I get a knot in my stomach before an exam.	
2. I feel nauseous before an exam.	
3. I get sweaty palms before an exam.	
4. I feel shaky before an exam.	
5. I have trouble sleeping the night before a test.	
6. My heart rate is increases before a test.	
7. I get pains in my neck and back prior to an exam.	
8. I lose my appetite before a test.	
9. I get headaches before a test.	
10. I feel fatigued before a test.	
11. I answer questions too fast.	
12. I make careless mistakes.	
13. I can't focus during the exam; my mind wanders.	
14. During the exam, I can't recall information I thought I knew.	
15. I worry about how everybody else is doing on the exam.	
16. I have difficulty understanding the test directions.	
17. I worry about past failures while taking tests.	

18. I feel like I am running out of time on tests, even though I still finish with time left over.	
19. I feel like I studied the wrong material before the test.	
20. After a test, I suddenly remember the correct answers.	

If you score between a 0-10, you do not have test anxiety. If you score an 11-20, you have mild test anxiety, which can be a healthy motivator and can easily be managed. If you score 21-40, you need to be aware of how testing anxiety can affect your performance and quality of life leading up to the exam. By using the strategies presented in this guide and seeking assistance, you can overcome even the most severe anxiety. Take a few minutes to carefully write down the causes of your anxiety. Then, review the guide to find possible strategies for overcoming your anxiety.

In what ways do I suffer from the most from testing anxiety?
A. _____
B. _____
C. _____
D. _____

What are some strategies to help me overcome this anxiety?
A. _____
B. _____
C. _____
D. _____

Examination Sub-Areas

Written Comprehension- understanding written English

Basic Arithmetic- addition, subtraction, multiplication, and division

Human Relations- The ability to apply common sense in challenging situations relating to teamwork and customer service skills. Includes deductive reasoning skills in terms of applying departmental rules and procedures to situational problems.

Mechanical Ability- The ability to understand how basic machines will operate. These questions require a basic understanding of levers, pulleys, and gears will work.

Reading Comprehension

This section of the exam has you read short sections of text and respond to questions about the text. The difficulty of the text closely matches that of what firefighters can expect on the job when reading manuals and department policy.

DISCLAIMER:

*The information contained in this segment is for test preparation only. It may contain inaccurate information and should not be relied upon as fact or actual operating procedures for any fire department. In no way, should this material be used for actual training purposes.

Reading Passage 1

Department operations procedure requires officers to make an immediate confidential medical evaluation and follow-up available for firefighters who have an exposure incident, such as a needlestick. An exposure incident is a specific eye, mouth, other mucous membrane, non-intact skin, or parenteral contact with blood or other potentially infectious materials (OPIM), as defined in the standard that results from the performance of a firefighter's duties.

Exposure incidents should be reported immediately to the officer since they can lead to infection with hepatitis B virus (HBV), hepatitis C virus (HCV), human immunodeficiency virus (HIV), or other bloodborne pathogens. When a firefighter reports an exposure incident right away, the report permits the department to arrange for an immediate medical evaluation of the firefighter. Early reporting is crucial for beginning immediate intervention to address possible infection of the firefighter and can also help the firefighter avoid spreading bloodborne infections to others. Furthermore, the department is required to perform a timely evaluation of the circumstances surrounding the exposure incident to find ways of preventing such a situation from occurring again. Reporting is also important because part of the follow-up includes identifying the source individual, unless the department can establish that identification is infeasible or prohibited by state or local law, and determining the source's HBV and HIV infectivity status. If the status of the source individual is not already known, the department is required to test the source's blood as soon as is feasible, provided the source individual consents. If the individual does not consent, the department must establish that legally required consent cannot be obtained. If state or local law allows testing without the source individual's consent, the department must test the individual's blood, if it is available. The results of these tests must be made available to the exposed firefighter, and the firefighter must be informed of the laws and regulations about disclosing the source's identity and infection status.

When a firefighter experiences an exposure incident, the department must make an immediate confidential medical evaluation and a follow-up available to the firefighter. This evaluation and follow-up must be: made available at no cost to the firefighter and at a reasonable time and place; performed by or under the supervision of a licensed physician or other licensed healthcare professional; and provided according to the recommendations of the U.S. Public Health Service (USPHS) current at the time the procedures take place. In addition, laboratory tests must be conducted by an accredited laboratory and must be at no cost to the firefighter. A firefighter who participates in post-exposure evaluation and follow-up may consent to have his or her blood drawn for determination of a baseline infection status, but has the option to withhold consent for HIV testing at that time. In this instance, the department must ensure that the firefighter's blood sample is preserved for at least 90 days in case the firefighter changes his or her mind about HIV testing. Post-exposure prophylaxis for HIV, HBV, and HCV, when medically indicated, must be offered to the exposed firefighter according to the current recommendations of the U.S. Public Health Service. The post-exposure follow-up must include counseling the firefighter about the possible implications of the exposure and his or her infection status, including the results and interpretation of all tests and how to protect personal contacts. The follow-up must also include evaluation of reported illnesses that may be related to the exposure.

Directions:

Base your answers to the following questions on the information provided in the reading passage above. *Do not base any answers on previous knowledge or experience.*

1. Whose responsibility is it to make an immediate confidential medical evaluation and a follow-up available when a bloodborne pathogen exposure has occurred?

A. firefighter

B. physician

C. department

D. officer

2. Bloodborne pathogens include all the following except:

A. HIV

B. HBV

C. HMV

D. HCV

3. Early reporting is crucial because it may allow:

A. the firefighter to avoid exposing others

B. the firefighter can begin a lawsuit sooner

C. the firefighter can completely avoid infection

D. the infection will be much less severe

4. After exposure is reported, the evaluation and follow-up must be:

A. made available for a fee to the firefighter and at a reasonable time and place

B. performed by or under the supervision of a licensed physician or other licensed healthcare professional

C. provided according to the recommendations of the department's current operating procedure at the time the procedures take place

D. made within 48 hours

5. The department must ensure that a firefighter's blood sample is preserved for:

A. 90 days

B. 60 days

C. 48 hours

D. for the career of the firefighter

6. Post-exposure follow-up must include:

A. all costs for treatment

B. counseling

C. prophylaxis

D. workmen's compensation

7. HCV is the pathogen that causes _____.

A. hepatitis B

B. hepatitis C

C. immunodeficiency disease

D. auto-immune disease

8. Post-exposure prophylaxis for HIV, HBV, and HCV, when medically indicated, must be offered to the exposed firefighter according to the current recommendations of the _____.

A. US Department of Health

B. the department

C. U.S. Public Health Service.

D. the healthcare provider who conducts the evaluation

9. An example of an exposure incident is

A. a needle-stick

B. being coughed on

C. shaking hands with an infected person

D. inhaling a droplet

10. A firefighter who participates in post-exposure evaluation and follow-up may consent to have his or her blood drawn for:

A. determining degree of infection

B. locating infection source

C. determination of a baseline infection status

D. locating other infected firefighters

Reading Passage 1 Answer Key:

1. D
2. C
3. A
4. B
5. A
6. B
7. B
8. C
9. A
10. C

Reading Passage 2

Firefighters who use extension ladders risk permanent injury or death from falls and electrocutions. These hazards can be eliminated or substantially reduced by following good safety practices. This operations manual examines some of the hazards firefighters may encounter while working on extension ladders and explains what the department and its firefighters can do to reduce risk of injuries.

What is an Extension Ladder? Also known as "portable ladders," extension ladders usually have two sections that operate in guides allowing for adjustable lengths. Because extension ladders are not self-supporting, they require a stable structure that can withstand the intended load.

Plan ahead to use the ladder safely

• Use a ladder that can sustain at least four times the maximum intended load (except that each extra-heavy duty type 1A metal or plastic ladder shall sustain at least 3.3 times the maximum intended load). Always follow the manufacturer's instructions on the ladder's label. To determine the correct ladder, consider your weight plus the weight of your load. Do not exceed the load rating, and always include the weight of all tools, materials and equipment.

• A qualified person must visually inspect all extension ladders before use for any defects such as: missing rungs, bolts, cleats, screws and loose components. If a ladder has these or other defects, it must be immediately marked as defective and sent to the maintenance division. Form 2012 must be completed by the officer in command; and, this form is to be sent to the quartermaster section.

• Allow sufficient room to step off the ladder safely. Keep the area around the bottom and the top of the ladder clear of equipment, materials and tools. If access is obstructed, secure the top of the ladder to a rigid support that will not deflect, and add a grasping device to allow firefighters safe access.

• Set the ladder at the proper angle. When a ladder is leaned against a wall, the bottom of the ladder should be one-quarter of the ladder's working length away from the wall. For access to an elevated work surface, extend the top of the ladder three feet above that surface or secure the ladder at its top.

• Before starting work, survey the area for potential hazards, (e.g. energized overhead power lines). Ladders shall have nonconductive side rails if they are used where the worker or the ladder could contact exposed energized electrical equipment. Keep all ladders and other tools at least 10 feet away from any power lines.

• Set the base of the ladder so that the bottom sits securely, and both side rails are evenly supported. The ladder rails should be square to the structure against which it is leaning with both footpads placed securely on a stable, level surface.

• Secure the ladder's dogs or pawls before climbing.

• When using a ladder in a high-activity area, secure it to prevent movement and use a barrier to redirect firefighters and equipment. If the ladder is placed in front of a door, always block off the door

Extension Ladders Safety Training:

Officers must train each firefighter to recognize and minimize ladder-related hazards.

FIREFIGHTERS MUST:

• Maintain a 3-point contact (two hands and a foot, or two feet and a hand) when climbing/descending a ladder.

• Face the ladder when climbing up or descending

• Keep the body inside the side rails

• Use extra care when getting on or off the ladder at the top or bottom. Avoid tipping the ladder over sideways or causing the ladder base to slide out.

• Carry tools in a tool belt or raise tools up using a hand line. Never carry tools in your hands while climbing up/down a ladder.

• Extend the top of the ladder three feet above the landing

• Keep ladders free of any slippery materials

FIREFIGHTERS MUST NOT:

• Place a ladder on boxes, barrels, or unstable bases

• Use a ladder on soft ground or unstable footing

• Exceed the ladder's maximum load rating

• Tie two ladders together to make them longer

• Ignore nearby overhead power lines

• Move or shift a ladder with a person or equipment on the ladder

• Lean out beyond the ladder's side rails

• Use an extension ladder horizontally like a platform

1. What is one hazard firefighters risk when using an extension ladder?

A. insect stings

B. pinched digits

C. muscle strains

D. electrocution

2. According to the presentation, hazards from using extension ladders can be reduced by:

A. constantly training

B. listening to officers

C. following the manufacturer's instructions

D. following good safety practices

3. An extension ladder is sometimes called a

A. portable ladder

B. step ladder

C. scaling ladder

D. pompier ladder

4. An extension ladder shall sustain at least _____ times the maximum intended load.

A. 2

B. 3.3

C. 4.3

D. 5.5

5. Where must defective ladders be sent?

A. quartermaster

B. officer in charge

C. maintenance division

D. headquarters

6. What form must be completed when a defective ladder is sent out?

A. 2020

B. 2010

C. 2012

D. 1220

7. Where is the form used for defective ladders sent?

A. quartermaster

B. officer in charge

C. maintenance division

D. headquarters

8. When a ladder is leaned against a wall, the bottom of the ladder should be _____ of the ladder's working length away from the wall.

A. ½

B. ¼

C. 2/3

D. ¾

9. Keep all ladders and other tools at least _____ away from any power lines.

A. 10 feet

B. 15 feet

C. 20 feet

D. 25 feet

10. When using a ladder do not:

A. Face the ladder when climbing up or descending

B. Keep the body inside the side rails

C. Extend the top of the ladder less than three feet above the landing

D. Keep ladders free of any slippery materials

Reading Passage 2 Answer Key:

1. D
2. D
3. A
4. B
5. C
6. C
7. A
8. B
9. A
10. C

Reading Passage 3

Chainsaw Use:

The chain saw is one of the most efficient portable power tools used for ventilation and rescue in firefighting. It can also be one of the most dangerous. If you learn to operate it properly and maintain the saw in good working condition, you can avoid injury as well as be more productive.

BEFORE STARTING THE SAW:

• Check controls, chain tension, and all bolts and handles to ensure they are functioning properly and adjusted according to the manufacturer's instructions

• Fuel the saw at least 10 feet from sources of ignition

• Check the fuel container for the following requirements:

-Must be metal or plastic

-Must not exceed a 5-gallon capacity

-Must be approved by the Underwriters Laboratory, Factory Mutual (FM), the Department of Transportation (DOT), or other Nationally Recognized Testing Laboratory.

WHILE RUNNING THE SAW:

• Keep hands on the handles, and maintain secure footing while operating the chainsaw

• Clear the area of obstacles that might interfere with cutting the tree or using the retreat path

• Do not cut directly overhead

- Shut off or release throttle prior to retreating

- Shut off or engage the chain brake whenever the saw is carried more than 50 feet, or across hazardous terrain

- Be prepared for kickback; use saws that reduce kickback danger (chain brakes, low kickback chains, guide bars, etc.). Personal Protective Equipment (PPE) for the head, ears, eyes, face, hands, and legs are designed to prevent or lessen the severity of injuries to firefighters using chain saws.

PERSONAL PROTECTIVE EQUIPMENT (PPE):

PPE must be inspected prior to use on each work shift to ensure it is in serviceable condition. The following PPE must be used when hazards make it necessary:

- head protection

- hearing protection

- eye/face protection

- leg protection

- foot protection

- hand protection

TRAINING:

Training requirements include:

- Specific work procedures, practices and requirements of the emergency scene, including the recognition, prevention, and control of general safety and health hazards

• Training should include material on bloodborne pathogens, first aid, and CPR.

• Instructions regarding ways to safely perform assigned work tasks, including the specific hazards associated with each task and the measures and practices which will be used to control those hazards.

• Procedures for to safe use, operation, and maintenance of tools, machines and vehicles which the firefighter will be required to utilize in completing the assigned requirements.

1. Fuel the saw at least _____ from sources of ignition.

A. 15 feet

B. 10 feet

C. 5 feet

D. 25 feet

2. A portable fuel tank…

A. may not be metal.

B. may not be plastic.

C. may be 6 gallons.

D. must not be approved by the Underwriters Laboratory, Factory Mutual (FM), the Department of Transportation (DOT), or other Nationally Recognized Testing Laboratory.

3. While using the chainsaw, do not...

A. clear the area of obstacles that might interfere with cutting the tree or using the retreat path.

B. cut directly overhead.

C. shut off or release throttle prior to retreating.

D. shut off or engage the chain brake whenever the saw is carried more than 50 feet, or across hazardous terrain.

4. Shut off or engage the chain brake whenever the saw is carried more than_____, or across hazardous terrain.

A. 50 feet

B. 10 feet

C. 25 feet

D. 100 feet

5. Chainsaw training should include material on all the following except:

A. bloodborne pathogens

B. first aid

C. CPR

D. violence prevention

6. All the following PPE must be used when hazards make it necessary:

A. head protection

B. hearing protection

C. groin protection

D. eye/face protection

7. PPE must be inspected prior to use _____ to ensure it is in serviceable condition.

A. on each work shift

B. daily

C. weekly

D. monthly

8. A use for a chainsaw is _____.

A. cutting firewood

B. forced entry

C. ventilation

D. automobile extrication

9. While using the saw, a firefighter should be prepared for:

A. flying debris

B. kickback

C. blade pinching

D. chain whip

10. When carrying the saw more than 50 feet, the firefighter should:

A. cover the blade

B. put the saw in a case

C. sling the saw

D. turn off the saw

Reading Passage 3 Answer Key:

1. B
2. C
3. B
4. A
5. D
6. C
7. A
8. C
9. B
10. D

Reading Passage 4

Sharpening a Chainsaw:

Sharpening a chainsaw is a necessary part of maintenance. Regular sharpening will make the saw cut more reliably and safely.

1. First, wear safety goggles and work gloves.
2. Select the correct diameter round file to suit the chain pitch. Consult the round file pitch guide to determine the correct diameter round file.
3. Use only special saw sharpening files.
4. Hold the file handle firmly with one hand, and guide the file with the other hand across the cutter on the forward stroke.
5. Start with the master cutter and position the file, so that you can apply pressure and file from the inside to the outside of the cutter.
6. Always hold the file at a right angle (90°) to the guide bar.
7. The file only sharpens on the forward stroke- lift the file off the cutter on the backstroke.
8. Rotate the file a little at regular intervals while filing to avoid one-sided wear.
9. Saw chains are designed to be filed to an angle of 30° parallel to the service mark.
10. Hold the file so that one quarter of its diameter projects above the top plate.
11. The cutting edge is properly sharpened when it is uniformly

bright.

12. File all cutters in the row the same depth, then turn the chainsaw 180° and file all the cutters in the other row. All cutters must be the same length as the master cutter.

13. The depth gauge setting becomes smaller when the cutter is sharpened.

14. After sharpening the cutters, check the depth gauge setting and lower it if necessary.

15. Place the filing gauge on the saw chain. If the depth gauge is higher than the filing gauge, it must be lowered.

16. File down the depth gauge until it is level with the filing gauge.

17. File the top of the depth gauge parallel to the service mark- but do not lower the highest point of the depth gauge in the process. Take care not to touch the freshly sharpened cutter with the flat file.

The risk of kickback is increased if the depth gauge is set too low.

1. What is the first step in sharpening a chainsaw?

A. checking depth gauge

B. selecting the file from the chart

C. wear goggles and gloves

D. testing saw

2. How do you select the proper round file?

A. ask the lieutenant

B. use the one that comes with the saw

C. use the depth gauge file

D. consult the round file pitch guide

3. The round file works on the _____.

A. forward stroke

B. back stroke

C. both back and forwards

D. on the diagonal

4. Start filing _____.

A. on the master cutter

B. on the master guide

C. any random place

D. on the depth guide

5. Hold the file at a _____ angle to the guide bar.

A. 15°

B. 30°

C. 90°

D. 180°

6. Saw chains are designed to be filed to an angle of _____ parallel to the service mark.

A. 15°

B. 30°

C. 90°

D. 180°

7. When done filing cutters on one side, rotate the saw _____.

A. 15°

B. 30°

C. 90°

D. 180°

8. Hold the file so that _____ of its diameter projects above the top plate.

A. ¼

B. ½

C. ¾

D. 1/8

9. The risk of kickback is increased if the depth gauge is set _____.

A. randomly

B. too high

C. too low

D. parallel to the cutter

10. File down the depth gauge until it is _____ with the filing gauge.

A. lower

B. higher

C. level

D. below

11. File the top of the depth gauge _____ to the service mark- but do not lower the highest point of the depth gauge in the process.

A. parallel

B. perpendicular

C. opposite

D. above

Reading Passage 4 Answer Key:

1. C
2. D
3. A
4. A
5. C
6. B
7. D
8. A
9. C
10. C
11. A

Reading Passage 5

Recharging a Water Fire Extinguisher:

Water fire extinguishers are very effective against small Class A fires and can be used for temporary suppression of larger fires. Class A fires are caused by a regular combustible such as paper or wood. It should not be used against an oil or grease fire because it may spread the fire. It should not be used against an electrical fire, because the water can conduct electricity and may electrocute the firefighter.

Complete the "Maintenance/Service Procedure" in order of items 1 through 11.

1. Discharge all remaining pressure and water making sure there is no remaining air pressure.

2. Remove the valve assembly and disassemble by removing downtube assembly (use a wrench on the brass retainer, not the plastic tube), spring and valve stem assembly. Remove collar O-ring from the valve and plastic fill tube from the cylinder.

3. Thoroughly rinse all parts with clean water and wipe dry with a soft cloth. Blow the valve out with air or nitrogen. Inspect the collar O-ring, valve stem and spring – replace parts if worn or damaged. Inspect the downtube. Replace it if it is cracked, deformed or does not have a threaded brass spring retainer. Inspect downtube O-ring, replace if necessary.

4. Rinse the cylinder with clean water and inspect the interior. Follow CGA Visual Inspection Standard C-6.

5. Firmly replace the plastic fill tube and fill cylinder with clean water until it overflows. Fill the unit with 2½ gallons of water.

6. Install a "Verification of Service" collar around the neck of the

cylinder. Install valve assembly to the cylinder and properly align. N.B. : Hand tighten the valve collar nut 100-125 in. lbs. Max (1.15 – 1.44 KG/m). Over-tightening with a wrench will damage the valve.

7. Remove cap from the air pressurizing valve on the side of the valve body and pressurize. Pressurize to 100 psi (690 kPa) using air or nitrogen. The pressure regulator should be set to no more than 125 psi (862 kPa). Replace pressure valve cap. The cap must be in place to ensure that valve will not leak.

8. Check the collar, gauge, air pressurizing valve, cylinder welds and valve orifice for leaks using leak detection fluid or a solution of soapy water. Remove leak detection fluid from the valve assembly by blowing out with air and wipe exterior of the extinguisher to dry.

9. Install hose and nozzle assembly.

10. Install ring pin with ring facing front of extinguisher. Install new tamper seal. Record recharge date and attach new recharge tag.

11. Weigh assembled extinguisher and confirm that the total weight is within the allowable tolerances indicated in the maintenance section on the extinguisher nameplate.

1. What is the next step after you have removed the valve stem assembly?

A. rinse the cylinder

B. remove collar O-ring

C. replace the plastic downtube

D. check the collar

2. According to the instructions, when should you replace the downtube?

A. when it is old

B. when the chrome plating has worn off

C. if it has a threaded brass retainer

D. if it is cracked

3. Where do you find the total weight specifications for the fire extinguisher?

A. in the manual

B. SOP bulletin

C. on the extinguisher nameplate

D. stamped on the extinguisher

4. What is the visual inspection standard for this piece of equipment?

A. 4-C

B. C-4

C. C-6

D. 6-C

5. How much water do you add to the extinguisher?

A. 1 gallon

B. 2 gallons

C. 2 ½ gallons

D. 4 gallons

6. On what class of fire do you use this extinguisher?

A. Class C

B. Class A

C. Class D

D. Class B

7. What is an example of a Class A fire?

A. paper

B. electrical

C. oil

D. grease

8. Where do you record the recharge date?

A. on the recharge tag

B. in the house log book

C. scribe it on the extinguisher base

D. on the rig's clipboard

9. What is the maximum pressure to which you can charge the extinguisher?

A. 50 psi

B. 75 psi

C. 100 psi

D. 125 psi

10. How much do you tighten the valve collar nut?

A. 100-125 ft. / lbs.

B. 100-125 inch / lbs.

C. 75ft. / lbs.

D. 150/ 175 ft. lbs.

Reading Passage 5 Answer Key:

1. B
2. D
3. C
4. C
5. C
6. B
7. A
8. A
9. D
10. B

Reading Passage 6

Emergency Care for a Choking Victim:

*If a victim CAN breathe, cough, or make sounds, then do not interfere.

If a conscious victim CANNOT breathe, cough or make sounds, ask if you can help.

If given consent by victim, give quick upward thrusts above the belly button and below the ribs until the object is forced out, victim can breathe again, or victim becomes unconscious.

For an unconscious victim, send someone to call 911 and get an automated external defibrillator (AED). If you are alone, perform 5 sets of 30 compressions and 2 breaths before leaving to call 911.

Follow these steps:

1. Give 30 compressions pushing down at least 2 inches on the center of the chest. Place one hand on top of the other. Push hard.

2. Open the airway and check for objects. Remove any obstructing object only you see.

3. With the airway, open, attempt to give two breaths. If unsuccessful, return to compressions.

Repeat steps 1, 2, and 3 until victim starts breathing or until emergency help arrives.

- Have someone call for an ambulance, rescue squad, or EMS.

- Do not practice on people. Abdominal thrusts may cause injury.

- Use back blows and chest thrusts on infants. Also, use chest thrusts on pregnant women and obese victims.

- For children 1 to 8 years of age, compress at a depth of approximately 2 inches.

- Perform emergency care for choking and cardiopulmonary resuscitation (CPR).

- For CPR training information, call your American Heart Association.

1. If a victim can cough:

    A. perform chest compressions

    B. do not interfere

    C. perform the Heimlich maneuver

    D. call 911

2. The first step after you determine a conscious victim is choking is to:

   A. start abdominal thrusts

   B. ask if you can help

   C. begin compressions

   D. call 911

3. The first step after you determine an unconscious victim is choking is to:

   A. start abdominal thrusts

   B. ask if you can help

   C. begin compressions

   D. send someone to call 911

4. If you are alone with an unconscious choking victim, before leaving to call 911, you should:

   A. perform 5 cycles of 30 chest compressions

   B. get the defibrillator

   C. perform abdominal thrusts

   D. do a blind finger sweep

5. On an unconscious adult, your compressions should go:

   A. approximately 2 inches deep

   B. at least 2 inches deep

   C. at least 1 ½ inches deep

   D. approximately 1 1/2 inches deep

6. When should you attempt to remove an object in a victim's airway?

   A. after every attempted breath

   B. before doing compressions

   C. after a blind finger sweep

   D. only if you see it

7. On an unconscious child 1-8 years of age, your compressions should go

   A. approximately 2 inches deep

   B. at least 2 inches deep

   C. at least 1 ½ inches deep

   D. approximately 1 1/2 inches deep

8. Who should you call for CPR training?

   A. the battalion chief

   B. your lieutenant

   C. Metrotech

   D. American Heart Association

9. What is the ratio of compressions to breaths for an adult victim and one rescuer?

   A. 15:2

   B. 5:1

   C. 30:2

   D. 15:1

10. For a choking infant use:

    A. compressions and thrusts

    B. abdominal thrusts only

    C. back blows and chest thrusts

    D. Heimlich maneuver

Reading Passage 6 Answer Key:

1. B
2. B
3. D
4. A
5. B
6. D
7. A
8. D
9. C
10. C

Reading Passage 7, Fall Protection Harness Inspection:

Fall protection harnesses are used in the construction industry and in rescue work. Fall protection harnesses differ from standard rescue harnesses in that they can absorb the energy produced in a fall, but can only absorb the energy from a fall once and then need to be removed from service. Regular inspection of the harness is necessary to ensure it works when needed.

Harness Inspection Guidelines:

Grasp the webbing with your hands and bend the webbing, checking both sides. This creates surface tension making damaged fibers or cuts easier to see. Webbing damage may not show up through a sight (visual) inspection only – manual (touch) inspection of the harness is equally important.

VISUAL AND TOUCH INSPECTION CRITERIA:

PASS

✓ Discoloration of material (dependent on cause of discoloration)

✓ Mildew (clean harness)

✓ Material marked w/ permanent marker (check w/ manufacturer)

✓ Discoloration of stitching (dependent on cause of discoloration)

FAIL

*Cuts, nicks or tears

*Broken fibers/cracks

*Overall deterioration

*Modifications by user

*Fraying/Abrasions

*Hard or shiny spots (indicates heat damage)

*Webbing thickness uneven (indicates possible fall)

*Missing straps

*Undue stretching (indicates possible fall)

*Burnt, charred or melted fibers (indicates heat damage)

*Excessive hardness or brittleness (indicates heat or UV damage)

*Pulled stitches

*Stitching that is missing

*Hard or shiny spots (indicates heat damage)

*Cut stitches

*Distortion (twists, bends)

*Rough or sharp edges

*Rust or corrosion

*Cracks or breaks

*Broken/distorted grommets

*Modification by users (i.e. additional holes)

*Tongue buckle should overlap the buckle frame and move freely back and forth

*Roller of tongue buckle should turn freely on frame

*Bars must be straight

*All springs must be in working condition

*Fall indicator activated (The fall indicator tab in the back of the harness will pull away when the force of a fall is applied).

Fall prevention harnesses should be removed from service if the user takes a fall while wearing it. The harness is designed to absorb the dynamic forces encountered in a fall and is sacrificed to protect the user. After the fall, the harness loses the ability to absorb the force encountered from subsequent falls. Snap hooks should be of the self-locking type. Snap hooks are proof tested to 3,600 lbs. and have minimum tensile strength of 5,000lbs.

Tagging System Inspection Guidelines:

Every harness must have a legible tag identifying the harness, model, date of manufacture, name of manufacturer, limitations and warnings.

1. Check tag for date of manufacture and remove from service, if past adopted service life (If tagging system is missing or not legible, remove harness from service).

2. Wipe off all surface dirt with a sponge dampened in plain water.

3. Squeeze the sponge dry.

4. Dip the sponge in a solution of water and mild detergent.

5. Work up a thick lather with a vigorous back and forth motion.

6. Wipe dry with a clean cloth.

7. Hang freely to dry but away from excessive heat, steam or long periods of sunlight.

8. Storage areas should be clean, dry, and free of exposure to fumes, heat, direct ultra violet light, sunlight, and corrosive elements.

Note: Do not store harnesses next to batteries, chemical attack can occur if battery leaks.

1. Why is manual inspection of the harness equally important as visual inspection?

A. webbing damage may not show up through a sight (visual) inspection only

B. touch is the best way

C. the harness may be used in darkness

D. light hides imperfections in the webbing

2. Which condition may result in a "PASS" of inspection?

A. bent bar

B. expired tag

C. discoloration

D. pulled stiches

3. While inspecting the webbing, what does bending it do?

A. pretensions the webbing

B. stretches the fibers

C. makes damaged fibers easier to see

D. makes broken grommets appear

4. The harness tag must identify all except:

A. model

B. date of manufacture

C. name of manufacturer

D. patent number

5. If the tag system is missing, the user should:

A. replace it when convenient

B. use it until a replacement can be found

C. remove it from service

D. inspect it and note date on tag to recertify it

6. What should the harness be cleaned with?

A. a bleach solution

B. an ammonia solution

C. a solution of water and mild detergent.

D. water only

7. The snap hook has a minimum tensile strength of
_____.

A. 1,000 lbs.

B. 3,000 lbs.

C. 5,000 lbs.

D. 3,500 lbs.

8. The snap hook has a minimum proof strength of _____.

A. 1,000 lbs.

B. 3,000 lbs.

C. 5,000 lbs.

D. 3,600 lbs.

9. Why should a harness be removed from service after a user falls while using it?

A. The harness is broken.

B. The harness absorbs the energy from the fall and loses the ability to absorb energy in subsequent falls.

C. The harness will break on the next fall.

D. The harness is only licensed for one time use.

10. How are fall protection harnesses different from standard rescue harnesses?

A. they are not as strong

B. they are stronger

C. they absorb the dynamic forces generated during a fall

D. they can be used for multiple falls

Reading Passage 7 Answer Key:

1. A
2. C
3. C
4. D
5. C
6. C
7. C
8. D
9. B
10. C

Reading Passage 8, Types of Fire Extinguishers:

A fire extinguisher is a storage container for an extinguishing agent (such as water or chemicals). It is designed to put out a small fire—not a big one. An extinguisher is labeled according to whether the fire on which it is to be used occurs in wood or cloth, flammable liquids, electrical, or metal sources. Using the wrong type of extinguisher on a fire can make the fire much worse.

The labels A, B, C, or D are used to indicate the type of fire on which an extinguisher is to be used. Most fire extinguishers will have a pictograph telling which classifications of fire the extinguisher is designed to fight. Pictures shown on the extinguisher in blue represent the type of fire on which an extinguisher is to be used. Pictures shown in black with a red slash across represent the type of fire on which the extinguisher is NOT to be used. For example, a simple water extinguisher should only be used on Class A fires.

CLASSIFICATION OF FUELS:

Fires are classified according to the type of fuel they burn. It is vitally important to always use the right type of fire extinguisher when putting out a small fire. If you use the wrong type of fire extinguisher on a mismatched class of fire, the fire may accelerate or spread. It is, therefore, very important to understand the four different fire classifications.

Class A (ordinary combustibles) - Class A fires involve solid combustible materials that are not metals such as wood, paper, textiles, and some plastics. Class A fires generally leave an ash.

Class B (flammable or combustible liquids & gases) - Class B fires involve flammable or combustible liquids and gases such as gasoline, diesel fuel, paint, paint thinners, and propane. Class B fires generally involve materials that boil or bubble.

Class C (energized electrical equipment) - If it is "plugged in" it would be considered a Class C fire. Examples include fires involving fuse boxes, circuit breakers, appliances, and machinery.

Class D (combustible metals) - Unless you work in a laboratory or in an industry that uses these materials, it is unlikely you must fight a Class D fire. Class D fires involve combustible metals including: sodium, potassium, magnesium, and titanium. These fires require special extinguishing agents (Metal-X, foam).

1. Fire extinguishers are classified by:

A. capacity

B. fire type

C. user

D. fire size

2. According to the lesson, using the wrong type of extinguisher can:

A. raise the cost of putting out the fire

B. damage property

C. cause the fire to spread

D. cause an explosion

3. Class A fires are caused by:

A. gasoline

B. cooking oil

C. paper

D. electricity

4. Class B fires are caused by:

A. gasoline

B. metals

C. paper

D. electricity

5. Class C fires are caused by:

A. gasoline

B. cooking oil

C. paper

D. electricity

6. Fires are classified by:

A. size

B. number of alarms

C. type of fuel

D. temperature

7. Pictures shown in black with a red slash indicate

A. fire type that extinguisher can put out the fire

B. the optimum type of extinguisher

C. size fire that can be put out

D. the type of fire that the extinguisher cannot be used on

8. An example of a combustible metal is:

A. sodium

B. aluminum

C. iron

D. steel

9. What extinguishing agents can be used on metal fires?

A. water

B. carbon dioxide

C. Metal-X

D. di-hydrogen oxide

Reading Passage 8 Answer Key:

1. B
2. C
3. C
4. A
5. D
6. C
7. D
8. A
9. C

Reading Passage 9, Inspecting a Fire Hydrant

1. It is recommended that hydrants be inspected (flushed) twice a year, spring and fall. After each use in extremely cold weather, hydrant should be checked specifically for drainage.

2. External Inspection:

a. Check chains to make sure they allow the nozzle cap to turn freely.

b. Check all caps to make sure they all can be removed.

c. Check paint and remove all lose paint (repaint if necessary).

3. Lubricate Hydrant Prior to Operating Hydrant:

a. Where oil is specified use white mineral oil USP. *Vegetable oil is not an acceptable substitute.*

b. Where grease is specified use food machinery grease.

4. Flushing Fire Hydrant:

a. Using a *hydrant operating wrench* turn the hydrant in the direction of opening indicated by an arrow cast in the hydrant. A pipe wrench is not the equivalent of a hydrant operating wrench.

b. Open hydrant at a moderate pace, typically one turn per second. It is not a race.

c. Open hydrant to FULL OPEN, it will come to solid stopping point. DO NOT try and open hydrant past this point. Damage can be done to the internal parts of the hydrant. If hydrant is not fully open water will flow out of drain or weep holes and cause damage to the drain field around the hydrant. Water may come up the sides of the hydrant or nearest valve box.

d. Flow hydrant until water becomes clear and no objects are flowing from the hydrant such as rocks. Be sure to control the direction of the flow of the hydrant so that damage is not done to anything in the water's path. Using some type of diffuser is recommended.

e. Close hydrant slowly, 1 turn every 1-2 seconds so that the hydrant does not close to quickly and create a water hammer that could possibly blow a water main.

f. When the hydrant is closed you should be able to back off the operating nut a quarter to half turn (sweet spot) water pressure should hold hydrant valve shut.

g. Place hand over nozzle and feel suction.

h. Leave nozzle cap off or loose to allow for hydrant to drain. Closing cap tightly before hydrant is drained will cause water to remain in hydrant barrel. In the winter this could freeze and cause the hydrant barrel to split or damaged internal parts of the hydrant. It could even possibly cause the hydrant to open itself up because of the weight of the ice in the barrel.

i. When hydrant has drained place small amount of food grade grease on nozzles and put on nozzle caps. Failing to routinely remove and grease nozzles could cause cap to rust to the nozzle and not allow the cap to be removed.

5. If hydrant fails to shut off, DO NOT force hydrant closed. Open hydrant back up and try to flush the obstruction out of the hydrant. It may take 3 to 4 attempts to flush out the obstruction. If this does not work, the hydrant must be taken apart for main valve and

possibly hydrant seat replacement.

6. If hydrant fails to drain, put all caps in place and tighten. Then open the hydrant 2 to 3 turns to attempt to flush out the drains of the hydrant. Let it sit in this open position for 5 to 10 minutes. Close hydrant and remove one of the caps to check for drainage. If hydrant still does not drain, it should be pumped after each use.

1. When should a hydrant be flushed?

A. once a year

B. after each fire

C. twice a year

D. each spring

2. What should you inspect regarding the chains?

A. that they are painted

B. that they allow the cover to rotate freely

C. that they are snug on the cap

D. that they prevent unauthorized access

3. What type of oil should be used to lubricate a hydrant?

A. vegetable oil

B. food service grease

C. white mineral oil

D. Vaseline

4. Which direction do you turn the wrench to open the hydrant?

A. right

B. left

C. in the direction of the arrow printed on the hydrant

D. in the direction opposite the arrow

5. How fast should you open a hydrant while flushing?

A. one rotation per second

B. one rotation per three seconds

A. one rotation per five seconds

D. two rotations per second

6. While flushing the hydrant, how long should you flush it for?

A. ten seconds

B. thirty seconds

C. Flow hydrant until water becomes clear, and no objects are flowing from the hydrant.

D. Flow hydrant until water becomes muddy, and objects are flowing from the hydrant.

7. If hydrant fails to drain,

A. put all caps in place and tighten.

B. let stand for 30 seconds.

C. open and close it several times.

D. shut it down tight.

8. If a hydrant fails to shut off,

A. open hydrant back up and try to flush the obstruction out of the hydrant.

B. shut it down tight.

C. tap the body of the hydrant with a sledge.

D. cover it with the caps.

Reading Passage 9 Answer Key:

1. C
2. B
3. C
4. C
5. A
6. C
7. A
8. A

Reading Passage 10

People first learn about fire as children. They know that fire consumes fuel, needs air, and gives off heat and light. Normally, that degree of understanding is more than sufficient. Firefighters, however, require a more nuanced understanding of the nature of fire. Specifically, they need a more extensive understanding of chemical processes, methods of heat transfer, the nature of fuels, and the environmental requirements for fire to occur. It is this knowledge that empowers firefighters to protect the community.

Foremost, fire is a by-product of a larger process called combustion. Typically, fire and combustion are two words interchangeably used by most people; notwithstanding, firefighters must understand the difference. Combustion is the self-sustaining process of the rapid oxidation of fuel producing heat and light. Fire is the result of a rapid combustion reaction.

IMPORTANT TERMS:

Flammable or Explosive Limits – the percentage of a substance (vapor) in air that will burn once it is ignited. Most substances have an upper (too rich) and a lower (too lean) flammable limit.

Flash Point – the minimum temperature at which a liquid fuel gives off sufficient vapor to form an ignitable mixture with air (typically near the liquids surface). At this temperature, the ignited vapor will flash, but it will not continue to burn.

Heat – the form of energy that raises temperature. Heat is measured by the amount of work it can do (e.g. the amount of heat needed to make a column of mercury expand inside a glass thermometer).

Ignition Temperature – the minimum temperature at which a fuel in air must be heated to start self-sustained combustion without a separate ignition source.

HEAT TRANSFER

Several natural laws of physics are involved in the transmission of heat. One is called the Law of Heat Flow; it specifies that heat tends to flow from a hot substance to a cold substance. The colder of two bodies will absorb the heat until both objects are at the same temperature. Heat can travel throughout a burning building by one, or more, of three methods: conduction, convection, and radiation.

Conduction

Heat may be conducted from one body to another by direct contact or by an intervening heat-conducting medium. An example of this type of heat transfer is a basement fire heating pipes, thereby, igniting the wood inside walls several rooms away. The amount of heat transferred (and its rate of travel) depends upon the conductivity of the material through which the heat is passing.

Not all materials have the same heat conductivity. Aluminum, copper, and iron are good conductors; however, fibrous materials, such as felt, cloth, and paper, are poor conductors. Liquids and gas are poor conductors of heat because of the movement of their molecules.

Air is also a relatively poor conductor. Double building walls and storm windows with airspace provide additional insulation from outside temperatures. Certain solid materials, such as fiberglass, shredded and packed, make good insulation, because the material itself is a poor conductor. The pockets of air within the batting act as insulation.

Convection

Convection is the transfer of heat via the movement of air or liquid. This movement is different from the molecular motion discussed in the conduction of heat. When liquids and gases are heated, they begin to move within themselves.

When water is heated in a glass container, the movement within the vessel can be observed through the glass. If sawdust is added to the water, the movement is more apparent. As the water is heated, it expands and grows lighter, hence, the upward movement.

In the same manner, when air near a steam radiator becomes heated by convection, it expands, becomes lighter, and moves upward. As the heated air moves upward, cooler air takes its place at the lower levels. For this reason, fire spread by convection is mostly in an upward direction; however, air currents have the potentiality to carry heat in any direction.

Convection currents are generally the cause of heat movement from floor to floor and from room to room. The spread of fire through corridors, up stairwells and elevator shafts; between walls, and through attics is caused mostly by the convection of heat currents. If heat convection encounters a ceiling keeping it from rising, it spreads out laterally (sideways) along the ceiling. If it runs out of ceiling space, it will travel down the wall toward the floor, being pushed by more heated air that is rising behind it. Convection encountering a ceiling is commonly referred to as mushrooming.

Convection has more influence upon fire attack and ventilation than either radiation or conduction. Although often mistakenly thought to be a separate form of heat transfer, direct flame contact is a form of convective heat transfer. When a substance is heated to the point where flammable vapors are given off, these vapors may be ignited, creating a flame. As other flammable materials meet the burning vapors, they may be heated to a temperature where they, too, will ignite and burn.

Radiation

Though a poor conductor, it is obvious that heat can travel through the atmosphere. The warmth of the sun reaches us even though it is not in direct contact (conduction) with the earth, nor is it heating up gases that travel through space (convection). The sun's method of heat transmission moves in waves and is known as radiation.

Heat and light waves are similar in nature, but they differ in length per cycle. Heat waves are longer than light waves, and they are sometimes called infra-red waves. Radiated heat will travel through space until it reaches an object with mass. As the object is exposed to heat radiation, it will reflect heat from its surface. Radiated heat is one of the major sources of fire, and its importance demands immediate attention at the location where radiant heat exposure is most severe.

1. The form of energy that raises temperature:

A. conduction

B. radiation

C. heat

D. convection

2. A form of heat transfer, whereby, one object is touching another:

A. conduction

B. radiation

C. heat

D. convection

3. A form of transfer where heat is driven by the movement of air or water:

A. conduction

B. radiation

C. heat

D. convection

4. A form of transfer where heat energy moves in waves:

A. conduction

B. radiation

C. heat

D. convection

5. An example of a good conductor is:

A. fiberglass

B. felt

C. paper

D. copper

6. An example of a poor conductor is:

A. aluminum

B. steel

C. paper

D. copper

7. The minimum temperature at which a liquid fuel gives off sufficient vapors to become ignitable:

A. flash point

B. flammable limit

C. heat

D. ignition temperature

8. The percentage of a substance (vapor) in the air that will burn once ignited:

A. flash point

B. flammable limit

C. heat

D. ignition temperature

9. The minimum temperature to which a fuel in air must be heated to start self-sustained combustion without a separate ignition source:

A. flash point

B. flammable limit

C. heat

D. ignition temperature

10. Fire is a by-product of a larger process called:

A. conduction

B. combustion

C. heat

D. convection

Reading Passage 10 Answer Key:

1. C
2. A
3. D
4. B
5. D
6. C
7. A
8. B
9. D
10. B

Reading Passage 11

For many years, the fire triangle (oxygen, fuel, and heat) was used to teach the components of fire. While this oversimplification is a useful teaching tool, it is technically not a complete picture. More accurately, for combustion to occur four components are necessary:

- Oxygen (oxidizing agent)
- Fuel
- Heat
- Self-sustained chemical reaction

These components are graphically depicted as the fire tetrahedron. Each component of the tetrahedron must be in place for combustion to occur. This concept is extremely important to students of fire suppression, prevention, and investigation. Remove any one of these four components and combustion will not occur. If ignition has already occurred, the fire is extinguished when one of the components is removed from the reaction.

Fuel may be found in three states of matter: solid, liquid, or gas. Only gases burn. The combustion of fuel requires the conversion of solids and liquids into a gaseous state by heating. Fuel gases are derived from solid fuels by pyrolysis. Pyrolysis is the chemical decomposition of a substance through the application of heat. Fuel gases are derived from liquids by vaporization.

This process is the same for water evaporating by boiling or in sunlight. In both cases, heat causes the liquid to vaporize. Generally, the vaporization process of liquid fuels requires less heat than pyrolysis – the process for solid fuels. This places considerable limitations on the control and extinguishment of liquid fuel fires, because their re-ignition is much more likely.

Gaseous fuels can be the most dangerous, because they are already in the natural state required for ignition. No pyrolysis or vaporization is needed to prime the fuel source. These fires are also the most difficult to contain.

1. What is missing from the fire triangle?

A. fuel

B. oxygen

C. heat

D. self-sustained chemical reaction

2. How many sides does a tetrahedron have?

A. five

B. three

C. four

D. six

3. What happens if one of the four components is removed from the combustion reaction?

A. explosion

B. acceleration

C. extinguished

D. vaporization

4. Out of the states of matter, which one can burn?

A. gas

B. liquid

C. plasma

D. solid

5. The initiation of the combustion of a liquid or solid fuel…

A. requires cooling

B. requires their conversion into a gaseous state by heating

C. requires a spark

D. requires molecular movement

6. The chemical decomposition of a substance through the action of heat is known as:

A. combustion

B. conduction

C. pyrolysis

D. vaporization

7. Fuel gases are evolved from liquids by the process of:

A. condensation

B. vaporization

C. pyrolysis

D. heating

8. Why are gaseous fuels typically more dangerous?

A. because they are already in the natural state required for ignition

B. because they are lighter

C. because they contain more energy

D. because they are more reactive

9. If any one of the four components of the fire tetrahedron are missing, what cannot occur?

A. explosion

B. convection

C. combustion

D. radiation

Reading Passage 11 Answer Key:

1. D
2. C
3. C
4. A
5. B
6. C
7. B
8. A
9. C

Reading Passage 12

Fires may start at any time of the day or night. If a fire occurs in an area protected by automatic suppression and detection systems, chances are that it will be discovered in the beginning (incipient) phase. When a building is closed, deserted, or without a fixed protection system, the fire may go undetected until it has gained major headway. The phase of a fire in a closed building is of chief importance when determining ventilation requirements.

Fire in a confined space has two particularly important characteristics. First, there is a limited amount of oxygen. This differs from an outdoor fire, where the oxygen supply is unlimited. The second characteristic is that the gases given off are trapped inside the structure and build up, unlike outdoors where they can dissipate. When a fire is confined in a building or room, the situation requires carefully thought-out and executed ventilation procedures, if further damage is to be prevented and danger reduced.

Fire confined to a building or room can be best understood by an investigation of its three main progressive phases: incipient, steady-state burning, and hot smoldering. A firefighter may be confronted by one or all the phases of fire at any one time; therefore, a working knowledge of these phases is important for understanding ventilation procedures. Firefighters must also be aware of the variety of potentially hazardous conditions that may be intertwined within the three main phases. These hazards include rollover, flashover, and backdraft.

Incipient Phase

The incipient phase is the earliest phase of a fire beginning with the actual ignition. The fire is limited to the original materials of ignition. In the incipient phase, the oxygen content in the air has not been significantly reduced, and the fire produces water vapor (H_2O), carbon dioxide (CO_2), a small quantity of sulfur dioxide (SO_2), carbon monoxide (CO), and other gases. Some heat is being generated, and the amount will increase as the fire progresses. The fire may be producing a flame temperature well above 1,000°F (537°C), yet the temperature in the room at this stage may only slightly increase.

Rollover

Rollover (sometimes referred to as flameover) takes place when unburned combustible gases released during the incipient (or early steady-state phase) accumulate at the ceiling level. These superheated gases are pushed, under pressure, away from the fire and into non-conflagrated areas mixing with oxygen. When their flammable range is reached, they ignite and a fire front develops, expanding very rapidly and rolling over the ceiling.

This is one of the reasons firefighters must stay low when advancing hose lines. Rollover differs from flashover in that only gases are burning (not the contents of the room). The rollover will continue until the fuel is eliminated. This is accomplished by extinguishing the main body of fire. The rollover will cease when the fire itself stops producing the flammable gases that are feeding it.

Steady-State Burning Phase

The steady-state burning phase (sometimes referred to as the free burning phase) is the phase of the fire during which sufficient oxygen and fuel are available for fire growth. At this stage, open burning progressing toward total involvement is possible. During the early portions of this phase, oxygen rich air is drawn into the flame, as convection (the rise of heated gases) carries the heat to the uppermost regions of the confined area. The heated gases spread out laterally from the top downward, forcing the cooler air to seek lower levels. Eventually, all combustible material in the upper levels of the room is ignited. This early portion of the steady-state burning phase is often called the flame-spread phase.

The presence of heated air is one of the reasons firefighters are taught to keep low and use protective breathing equipment. One breath of superheated air will sear the lungs. At this point, temperature in the upper regions can exceed 1,300°F (700°C). If conditions are perfect the fire may achieve a state of "clear burning." Clear burning is accompanied by high temperatures and complete combustion. Little or no smoke is given off. Clear burning only occurs when very clean fuels, such as methanol-based race car fuels, ignite.

Thermal columns normally occur with rapid air movement upward from the base of the fire. As the fire progresses (in a confined space) through the latter portions of the steady-state burning phase, the fire continues to consume the free oxygen. Eventually, the fire reaches a point at which there is insufficient oxygen to react with the fuel. The fire is then reduced to the smoldering phase. However, the fire only needs a fresh supply of oxygen to begin to burn rapidly.

Flashover occurs when flames engulf the entire surface of a room. The underlying cause of flashover is the contained buildup of heat from the confined fire. As the fire continues to burn, all the contents of the room area are gradually heated to their ignition temperatures. When reaching their ignition point, simultaneous ignition occurs, and the area becomes fully involved in fire. This ignition is virtually instantaneous and can be quite dramatic. A flashover can usually be avoided by directing water toward the ceiling level and the room contents to cool materials below their ignition temperatures.

Hot Smoldering Phase

After the steady-state burning phase, flames may be extinguished, if the area of confinement is sufficiently airtight. In this instance, burning is reduced to glowing embers. As the flames die down, the room becomes filled with dense smoke and gases. Air pressure may build to the extent that smoke and gases are forced through small cracks. Room temperatures more than 1,000°F (370°C) are possible.

The intense heat will have liberated the lighter fuel fractions, such as methane, from the combustible material in the room. Lighter fuel gases are produced during smoldering and further increase the hazard to the firefighter. Furthermore, there exists the possibility of a backdraft, if air is improperly introduced into the room. The fire will eventually burn itself out, leaving totally incinerated contents, if air is not reintroduced to the room.

Firefighters responding to a confined fire late in the steady-state burning phase or in the hot smoldering phase risk causing a backdraft (also known as a smoke explosion). A backdraft is among the most hazardous conditions firefighters encounter. In the hot-smoldering phase, burning is incomplete because of insufficient oxygen to sustain the fire. However, the heat from the steady state burning phase remains, and the carbon particles and other flammable products for combustion are available for instantaneous reignite the fire.

When more oxygen is supplied, such as opening a door or breaking a window, the dangerous missing link, oxygen, is added. As soon as the needed oxygen rushes in, the stalled combustion resumes; it can be devastating in its speed - truly qualifying as an explosion.
Questions:

1. The earliest phase of a fire is called:

A. incipient phase

B. backdraft

C. rollover

D. steady-state burning phase

2. During the incipient phase,

A. fire is limited to the original materials of ignition.

B. rollover occurs.

C. backdraft re-ignites the fire.

D. the fire burns in a free-burning state.

3. This phase occurs when superheated gases reach their flammable range and mix with oxygen:

A. incipient

B. backdraft

C. rollover

D. superheating

4. Another term for the steady-state burning phase is:

A. free-burning

B. backdraft

C. latent

D. incipient

5. The steady-state phase is best described as:

A. fire limited to the original materials of ignition

B. fire with sufficient oxygen and fuel available for growth and open burning to a point where total involvement is possible

C. the stage where flames may cease to exist, if the area of confinement is sufficiently airtight and glowing embers remain

D. the flare-up resulting from rapid re-introduction of oxygen to combustion in an oxygen depleted environment

6. The hot-smoldering phase is:

A. the phase where fire is limited to the original materials of ignition

B. the phase of the fire where sufficient oxygen and fuel are available for fire growth and open burning to a point where total involvement is possible

C. the phase where flames may cease to exist, if the area of confinement is sufficiently airtight and glowing embers remain

D. the result of rapid re-introduction of oxygen to combustion in an oxygen depleted environment

7. Backdraft is known as:

A. the stage where fire is limited to the original materials of ignition

B. the phase where sufficient oxygen and fuel are available for fire growth and open burning to a point where total involvement is possible

C. the phase where flames may cease to exist, if the area of confinement is sufficiently airtight and glowing embers remain

D. a rapid flare up from rapid re-introduction of oxygen to combustion in an oxygen-depleted environment

8. During the hot-smoldering phase, room temperatures in excess of _____ may be reached.

A. 1,000°F

B. 1,300 °F

C. 537 °F

D. 700°F

9. During the incipient phase, the fire may produce flames well in excess of:

A. 1,000°F

B. 1,300 °F

C. 537 °F

D. 700°F

10. During the steady-state burning phase, temperatures in the upper area can reach:

A. 1,000°F

B. 1,300 °F

C. 537 °F

D. 700°F

Reading Passage 12 Answer Key:

1. A

2. A

3. C

4. A

5. B

6. C

7. D

8. A

9. A

10. B

Reading Passage 13

Ladder Company Operations

First Ladder Company (order of operations):

1. Ladder company begins operations on fire floor

2. Determine life hazard and rescue as required

3. Roof ventilation and a visual check of rear and sides from this level

4. Laddering as needed

5. If second ladder company will not arrive within a reasonable time, make interior search and removal of endangered occupants above the fire

Second Ladder Company (order of operations):

1. Go to all floors above the fire floor for search, removal, ventilation and to check for fire extension

2. Confirm roof ventilation (assist first unit)

3. Check rear and sides of buildings

4. Reinforce laddering and removal operations when necessary

The department has specific procedures for the following types of buildings: taxpayer buildings, row frame buildings, brownstones, private dwellings, vacant buildings, high rise office buildings and fireproof multiple dwellings. Ladder companies institute a two-team offensive to cover their assigned area of responsibility. The content below outlines the tools, positions and duties for each member of the first and second ladder companies arriving at a fire at a non-fireproof multiple dwelling. The ladder company members' tools, positions and duties vary depending on the type of building.

Non-fireproof multiple dwellings represent the bulk of the department's responses.

Non-Fireproof Ladder Company Protocol:

INSIDE TEAM	OUTSIDE TEAM:
• Officer	• Chauffeur
• Forcible entry position (IRONS)	• Outside Vent (OV)
• Extinguisher position (CAN)	• Roof

Basic Equipment complement for ladder company personnel

- Basic bunker gear - 19.5 lbs. (coat, pants, boots, gloves, and hood)
- Helmet - 3.5 lbs.
- SCBA (Self-Contained Breathing Apparatus) -27.5 lbs. (45 min. cylinder)
- PSS (Personal Safety System) -6 ¾ lbs. (includes harness)
- Radio-1 ¼ lbs. (includes battery & harness)
- Light- 3 lbs.
- Tools-1 to 3 lbs. (knife, wrench, screw driver, chock)
- Total weigh t- 62 ½ -65 ½ lbs.

1. The second operation of the first ladder company is:

A. ladder company operations on fire floor

B. determine life hazard and rescue as required

C. roof ventilation and a visual check of rear and sides from this level

D. laddering as needed

2. The second operation of the second ladder company is:

A. ladder company operations on fire floor

B. determine life hazard and rescue as required

C. roof ventilation and a visual check of rear and sides from this level

D. confirm roof ventilation (assist first unit)

3. The first operation the second ladder company is:

A. Go to all floors above the fire floor for search, removal, ventilation and to check for fire extension.

B. determine life hazard and rescue as required

C. roof ventilation and a visual check of rear and sides from this level

D. confirm roof ventilation (assist first unit)

4. What type of building make up the bulk of department responses?

A. non-fireproof multiple dwellings

B. single family homes

C. office buildings

D. industrial properties

5. Who is a member of the inside team?

A. chauffer

B. officer

C. roof

D. outside vent

6. What piece of equipment is not part of bunker gear?

A. coat

B. pants

C. boots

D. helmet

7. How much does SCBA weigh?

A. 19.5 lbs.

B. 27.5 kg.

C. 19.5 kg.

D. 27.5 lbs.

8. If the second ladder company will not arrive in a reasonable amount of time, then the first ladder company should...

A. perform interior search and removal of endangered occupants above the fire.

B. confirm roof ventilation (assist first unit).

C. check rear and sides of buildings.

D. reinforce laddering and removal operations when necessary.

9. How much does the basic equipment carried by ladder personnel weigh?

A. 62 ½ -65 ½ kgs.

B. 62 ½ -65 ½ lbs.

C. 52 ½ - 55 ½ lbs.

D. 62- 65 lbs.

10. How long is the SCBA tank designed to last for?

A. 10 minutes

B. 47 minutes

C. 27.5 minutes

D. 45 minutes

Reading Passage 13 Answer Key:

1. B

2. D

3. A

4. A

5. B

6. D

7. D

8. A

9. B

10. D

Reading Passage 14

Taxpayer Store Fire Protocol (First Ladder Company):

INSIDE TEAM

Position:

- The store occupancy involved with fire

Duties:

- Forcible entry

- Locate the fire

- Provide and maintain an unobstructed path through which the hose line can advance

- Open ceilings, ducts and partitions

- Cellar fires might require the cutting of floors for ventilation & operation of cellar pipes, distributors, bent tips or high expansion FOAM

- Search & removal of victims

- Ventilate as required in order to conduct this search

- Shut down utilities

Tool Assignments:

"Can" Firefighter

- 6 ft. hook
- Pressurized water extinguisher

"Irons" Firefighter

- Axe & Halligan (or maul & Halligan)
- Rabbit tool (hydra ram)
- Security doors may dictate specialized equipment i.e. forcible entry saw (aluminum oxide blade), duckbill, maul, etc.

OUTSIDE TEAM

Outside Vent (OV) Firefighter

Position:

- Check the rear and sides

Duties:

- Provide ventilation at the rear
- Enter and search teamed up with another firefighter

Tool assignments:

- Maul & Halligan

Roof Firefighter

Position:

- Roof of fire building via a portable ladder

Duties:

- Vertical ventilation (scuttles, skylights, etc.)

- Communicate conditions found, e.g. location or extension of fire or heavy equipment on roof

Tool Assignment:

- 6 ft. hook, Halligan

- For fires above the cellar, the saw and hook are taken

Chauffeur Firefighter:

Position:

- if tower ladder, position it in front of the building

- if an aerial ladder, place it away from the immediate front to leave area accessible for a tower ladder

Duties:

- join forcible entry team

- if fire extends to the cockloft, proceed to the roof and assist the roof firefighter

1. The 1st ladder company to arrive (inside team) should be positioned:

A. on roof

B. on side of building

C. next to fire building

D. the store occupancy involved in the fire

2. A duty of the inside team is:

A. check the rear and sides

B. provide ventilation at the rear

C. enter and search teamed up with another firefighter

D. complete forcible entry

3. A duty of the roof personnel is:

A. check the rear and sides

B. provide vertical ventilation

C. enter and search teamed up with another firefighter

D. complete forcible entry

4. A tool assigned to the outside ventilation personnel is

A. rabbit tool

B. hydraulic ram

C. maul

D. 6 ft. hook

5. A tool only assigned to inside team personnel is

A. rabbit tool

B. hydraulic ram

C. maul

D. 6 ft. hook

6. How is the roof of the taxpayer building accessed by the roof personnel?

A. tower ladder

B. staircase

C. portable ladder

D. fire escape

7. If the fire extends to the cockloft, the chauffer should...

A. proceed to the roof and assist the roof firefighter.

B. move the apparatus to the rear of building.

C. assist the inside team.

D. prepare for evacuation of roof firefighter.

8. Specialized equipment for a steel security door includes:

A. rabbit tool

B. portable extension ladder

C. duckbill

D. Halligan tool

9. Where should a tower ladder be positioned by the chauffer?

A. Position it in front of the building.

B. Place it away from the immediate front of the building.

C. Position it in the rear of the building.

D. Position it on the side.

10. For a fire above the cellar, the roof firefighter should take:

A. the Halligan tool

B. the saw and hook

C. the rabbit tool

D. the duckbill

Reading Passage 14 Answer Key:

1. D

2. D

3. B

4. C

5. A

6. C

7. A

8. C

9. A

10. B

Number Facility

Number facility is the ability to complete numerical operations including addition, subtraction, division and multiplication. This section tests the speed of computation in addition to accuracy.

SAMPLE QUSTIONS:

Please use the following information to calculate the correct answers.

1. A fire vehicle has an average range of 420 miles on a full tank of gas. The gauge reads one quarter (1/4) of a tank. How far will the vehicle be able to drive?

A. 105 miles
B. 210 miles
C. 315 miles
D. 400 miles

2. Captain Jones needs to measure the rectangular equipment room. She uses measuring tape to find the south wall which is 18 feet in length and the east wall which is 15 feet long. What is the area of the equipment room?

A. 270 sq. ft.
B. 360 sq. ft.
C. 180 sq. ft.
D. 90 sq. ft.

Answers:

1. A
2. A

Number Facility Practice Questions

1. 22 X 11=

A. 242
B. 133
C. 2211
D. 222

2. 575/ 5=

A. 131
B. 2525
C. 250
D. 115

3. If a firefighter works 8 hours on Monday, 8 hours on Tuesday, 16 hours on Wednesday, 16 hours on Thursday, and 8 hours on Friday, how many hours did he work that week?

A. 56
B. 66
C. 54
D. 46

4. A firefighter's rate of pay is $40.00 per hour. She earns time and a half for overtime and works 20 hours of overtime in each week. What would be her total pay for the overtime hours worked?

A. $800
B. $1,000
C. $1,200
D. $1,600

5. A probationary firefighter has $100 in his savings account. He purchases twenty Ramen Noodle packs at $0.50 per package. He also purchases 16 cans of tuna fish at $1.50 per pack. How much money will he have left in his account?

A. $56
B. $66
C. $36
D. $34

6. A probationary firefighter completes 150 pushups a day for 30 days. How many pushups did she complete in total?

A. 450
B. 4500
C. 1500
D. 350

7. Rules require that there are 3 officers for every 25 trainees. Currently there are 2025 trainees at the facility. How many officers are required?

A. 243
B. 2430
C. 234
D. 2340

8. According to the fire code, a preschooler must have 25 sq. feet of space in a classroom. There are 10 preschoolers in a classroom. How much space is required?

A. 25
B. 200
C. 250
D. 220

9. A trainee arrives at the training facility weighing 180 pounds. After a month, he now weighs 162 pounds. What percentage of bodyweight did the he lose?

A. 5%
B. 10%
C. 15%
D. 20%

10. After 20 years, a firefighter can retire with a pension of 50% of her final salary. Firefighters then accrue 2% per year for each additional year. If that firefighter works for 30 years, what percentage of her final salary will her pension be?

A. 55%

B. 60%

C. 70%

D. 80%

Answers: 1. A, 2. D, 3. A, 4. C, 5. B, 6. B, 7. A, 8. C, 9. B, 10. C

Mathematical Reasoning

Mathematical reasoning is the ability to apply logic abstractly using quantitative concepts and symbols. It encompasses reasoning through mathematical problems to determine the appropriate operations to be performed to solve a given problem. It also includes the structuring of mathematical equations. The actual computation of the numbers is not necessarily included in this ability.

SAMPLE QUESTIONS:

Please use the following information to answer the sample questions.

When responding to a fire, the department must adjust its number of firefighters to the number of alarms. The table below shows the suggested number of firefighters needed to respond to a fire.

Number of Alarms	Number of Firefighters Required
1	9
2	18
3	27
4	36

A. As the number of alarms increases, the number of firefighters required on the scene triples.

B. As the number of alarms increases, the number of firefighters required on the scene decreases.

C. The number of firefighters required on the scene increases at the same rate as the number of alarms.

D. As the number of alarms increases, the number of firefighters required on the scene also increases at a constant rate.

Correct Answer is **D**. For each alarm, nine firefighters are required to respond.

To reduce rescue time, the Department has instituted a study to determine the correct staffing numbers for vehicle extractions. The table below shows the results of this investigation.

Which statement most accurately reflects the results of the investigation?

Firefighters Assigned	Time for Extraction
9	25
14	20
19	15
24	10
29	5

A. For every five firefighters added, the number of minutes decreased by 5.

B. As the number of firefighters increased, the time decreased disproportionately.

C. As the number of firefighters increased, the time decreased exponentially.

D. For every five firefighters added, the time was cut in half.

Correct Answer is **A**. For each five firefighters added, the time decreased by 5 minutes.

Mathematical Reasoning Practice Set

1. Jones is twice as old as his friend Frank. Frank is 5 years older than Ortiz. In 5 years, Jones will be three times as old as Ortiz. How old is Jones?

A. 8 years' old
B. 12 years old
C. 14 years old
D. 10 years old

2. Marcus' dad is 4 times older than Marcus, and Marcus is twice as old as his sister Gina. In three years, the sum of their ages will be 42. How old is Marcus now?

A. 6 years old
B. 7 years old
C. 8 years old
D. 9 years old

3. Michael scored 67, 77, 81, 75, and 82 on his mathematical reasoning exams. What will be his average grade in mathematical reasoning from this exam?

A. 77.2
B. 76.4
C. 78.1
D. 75.5

4. Roberta left work and drove at the rate of 35 miles per hour for 2 hours. She stopped for breakfast then drove for another 2 hours at a speed of 55 mph to reach training in Albany. How many miles did Roberta drive to reach Albany?

A. 110 miles
B. 70 miles
C. 90 miles
D. 180 miles

5. Diamond went to Quartermaster Supply, Inc. She bought a new duty belt and a pair of Class "A" uniform shoes. The shoes were on sale for 20% off. She paid $80.00. What was the original price of the shoes?

A. $105.60
B. $66.00
C. $102.00
D. $108.00

6. If Sapphire's weekly income doubled, she would be making $60 a week more than Jamie. Sapphire's weekly income is $80 more than half of Francis'. Francis makes $400 a week. How much does Jamie make?

A. $160
B. $400
C. $550
D. $500

7. A conference with 2000 participants gathers in the Bronx. One out of every five people attending the conference who have ordered meals requested Halal food. 25% of those attending the conference signed up for meals. How many requested Halal?

A. 150
B. 125
C. 100
D. 200

8. There is a uniform allowance of $180 per firefighter for every six months. At this same rate, what would the uniform allowance be for 10 firefighters for a period of 12 months??

A. $1800
B. $2800
C. $2700
D. $3600

9. In October, the Manhattan South Battalion spent $88000, or 20% of its personnel expenses that month on overtime. What were its total personnel expenses for the month of October?

A. $44,000
B. $880,000
C. $440,000
D. $4,400,000

10. Firefighter Caldwell bought an equal number of $12.00, $8.00, and $6.00 duty socks for his uniform. He spent $130 for all of the socks. How many of each did he buy?

A. 7

B. 9

C. 5

D. Cannot be determined from information given

Answers: 1. D, 2. A, 3. B, 4. D, 5. A, 6. D, 7. C, 8. D, 9. C, 10. C

Human Relations

The expectation on this exam is that firefighters behave in a professional manner. The creators of the exam make no distinction from firefighting and office work. This is why so many experienced firefighters have difficulty answering the questions on this section of the exam. When answering these questions, ask yourself "What would I do if I was working in a bank and was confronted with this situation". This test is not based on the reality of typical behavior in a firehouse or department. The gallows humor, banter, and hazing that the public associates with firehouse life is deemed unacceptable by the producers of the exam. The following is a guide as to how to respond to the human relations question set.

How do you decide when it is appropriate to inform an officer about the behavior of another firefighter?

1. If the behavior is dangerous.

Ex. A fellow firefighter is drunk while on duty, or using illegal or mind altering drugs.

2. If the behavior threatens the integrity of the department or the unit.

Ex. A fellow firefighter is stealing property from a fire scene, or using sick time to go on vacation.

3. If the behavior constitutes sexual harassment.

Every professional fire department should be a workplace that is free from sexual harassment. Sexual harassment in the workplace is against the law and should not be tolerated. When a department determines that an allegation of sexual harassment is credible, it must take prompt and appropriate corrective action.

What Is Sexual Harassment?

Unwelcome sexual advances, requests for sexual favors, and other verbal or physical conduct of a sexual nature constitute sexual harassment when:

1) An employment decision affecting that individual is made because the individual submitted to or rejected the unwelcome conduct; or

2) The unwelcome conduct unreasonably interferes with an individual's work performance or creates an intimidating, hostile, or abusive work environment.

Certain behaviors, such as conditioning promotions, awards, training or other job benefits upon acceptance of unwelcome actions of a sexual nature, are always wrong.

Unwelcome actions such as the following are inappropriate and, depending on the circumstances, may in and of themselves meet the definition of sexual harassment or contribute to a hostile work environment:

- Sexual pranks, or repeated sexual teasing, jokes, or innuendo, in person or via e-mail;
- Verbal abuse of a sexual nature;
- Touching or grabbing of a sexual nature;
- Repeatedly standing too close to or brushing up against a person;
- Repeatedly asking a person to socialize during off-duty hours when the person has said no or has indicated he or

she is not interested (supervisors should be careful not to pressure their employees to socialize);

- Giving gifts or leaving objects that are sexually suggestive;
- Repeatedly making sexually suggestive gestures;
- Making or posting sexually demeaning or offensive pictures, cartoons or other materials in the workplace;
- Off-duty, unwelcome conduct of a sexual nature that affects the work environment.

A victim of sexual harassment can be a man or a woman. The victim can be of the same sex as the harasser. The harasser can be a supervisor, co-worker, other department employee, or a non-employee who has a business relationship with the department.

If your exam presents a scenario where any of the above conditions describing sexual harassment occur, the best choice is to report the incident to an officer, and follow the chain of command until the matter is appropriately resolved. The worse choice in this scenario is to ignore the harassment. Ignoring the harassment will only allow it to escalate and puts the entire department at risk.

Think about it in these terms: If there is something that is going on that can threaten the department or cause injury to a member or the public, you have an obligation to inform the officer and let them decide how to deal with the issue. Keeping the officer in the dark leaves the entire department vulnerable.

Times when you would not inform an officer would be matters that are more trivial such as cleaning duties, simple misunderstandings, and minor scheduling conflicts. Keep in mind that there is an expectation that entry level firefighters arrive early, stay late, are eager to learn, and stay busy cleaning and maintaining the firehouse.

How should you deal with hygiene, housekeeping, and issues concerning personal property?

You will most likely get a question set dealing with a firefighter who leaves dishes, overuses laundry facilities, or fails to pull their weight with cooking or housekeeping duties. Most of these issues can be dealt with using clear communication. If somebody does something that is minor or irritating, it is best to address it privately and clearly. If it is a one-time occurrence, with no risk of injury or damage to department integrity, it is best to let the matter go. If the matter persists, then address it directly, but with tact and without aggression.

Think about the difference between being assertive versus being aggressive.

It is alright to stand up for yourself, but your response should be to diffuse conflict and de-escalate the situation.

The best option for these types of questions is to go to the source of the issue, when appropriate, and use tact to rectify the situation. The worst course of action will lead to further conflict and escalation.

What do you do if you have been assigned to a task by one officer, and another officer gives you a different or contradictory order?

Your solution here is to communicate with both officers. Your obligation is to acknowledge the order and then explain that you were previously ordered to do a different task. By informing both officers, the higher-ranking officer can then decide the best course of action and alleviate you of this burden. You must keep in mind never to refuse an order outright, which would be insubordination.

Example: You have been assigned to clean the irons after returning to the house after a fire by Lt. Smith. Captain Jones walks up and orders you to complete form 2211. You state "Yes Sir. Lt. Smith ordered me to clean the irons. May I inform him that you need me to complete the form first, and then return to the irons." If the captain says "yes" to your request, you are clear. If he says "no", you are also clear, because you requested permission to tell Lt. Smith and you were denied. The key here is communication. If you just left the irons and didn't ask the captain permission to tell the Lt., you would be in trouble because neither officer would understand.

If the matter were more pressing in nature, you would not have the time to return to the first officer. You would still have the obligation to inform the officer in front of you what your prior directive was.

Example: Lt. Jones instructed you to vent the roof of a house. The conditions change and Captain Smith instructs you to hold off. Your obligation would be to say "Yes sir, Lt. Jones instructed me to vent, but I am holding off awaiting your further instruction." In this way, you have acknowledged the Captain's command, informed him of your prior directive, and stated your next course of action, which is awaiting further orders. If Lt. Jones asks you why you haven't vented the roof, you inform him that Captain Jones was aware of the order, but instructed you to hold off.

What is a paramilitary organizational structure?

Most fire departments are structured with entry level firefighters at the bottom. The next level is the Lieutenant who is considered an officer. Lieutenants are typically in charge of several firefighters and a piece of apparatus. Next is the Captain who oversees a team of firefighters, a piece of apparatus, and is the highest-ranking officer in a fire house. A chief oversees a department and will generally run a fire as the commanding officer. The commissioner is typically a civilian who is in an elected or appointed position. The commissioner typically works to set policy, budget, and handles administrative issues. In many municipalities, professional firefighters hold a 'Peace Officer' status and have the authority to issue summonses for violations of building and fire codes.

How does the chain of command relate to this part of the exam?

In the context of a fire department, the chain of command is the line of authority and responsibility along which orders are passed within the department and between different units within the department. Orders are transmitted down the chain of command, from a higher-ranked officer, such as a captain or chief, to lower-ranked firefighters who either execute the order personally or transmit it down the chain as appropriate, until it is received by those expected to execute it.

In general, firefighting personnel give orders only to those directly below them in the chain of command and receive orders only from those directly above them. A member who has difficulty executing a duty or order and appeals for relief directly to an officer above his immediate commander in the chain of command is likely to be disciplined for not observing the chain of command. Similarly, an officer is usually expected to give orders only to his or her direct subordinate, even if it is just to pass an order down to another service member lower in the chain of command than said subordinate.

The concept of chain of command also implies that higher rank alone does not entitle a higher-ranking service member to give commands to anyone of lower rank. For example, an officer of Engine Company 123 does not directly command lower-ranking members of Ladder Company 456, and is generally expected to approach an officer of Ladder 456 if he requires action by members of that company. The chain of command means that individual members take orders from only one superior and only give orders to a defined group of people immediately below them.

Example: If an officer of Engine Company 123 does give orders directly to a lower-ranked member of Ladder 456, it would be considered highly unusual (such as emergency circumstances, a lack of time or inability to communicate with the officer in command of Ladder Company 456) as the officer of Engine Company 123 would be subverting the authority of the officer of Ladder Company 456. Depending on the situation or the standard procedure of the Department, the lower-ranked member being ordered may choose to carry out the order anyway, or advise that it must be cleared with his or her own chain of command first, which in this example would be with the officer of Ladder Company 456. Refusal to carry out an order is almost always considered insubordination, the only exception usually allowed is if the order itself is illegal (i.e., the person carrying out the order would be committing an illegal act).

What do you do if you do not understand an order or how to do something?

The best course of action is to ask for clarification form the person instructing you. If you still don't understand, ask again. Lives are at risk if you don't understand how to use a piece of equipment or know how to perform a procedure. You may have to swallow some pride, but the correct course here is to make sure you understand.

Going to a senior firefighter for clarification is second best. Worst would be asking another probationary firefighter or figuring it out on your own later. It is expected that an entry level firefighter will need to learn a great deal and will normally have some difficulty with challenging topics or procedures. The test is most concerned with how a recruit approaches learning and deals with the challenges presented.

What do you do if confronted by a member of the press about a fire or the condition of a victim?

As an entry level firefighter, you do not have the authority to speak on behalf of the Department unless expressly given permission to do so by the leadership of the Department. Your job here is to politely refer all questions to the ranking officer present. You may get a question about a phone call coming into the firehouse while the officer is engaged in some other important work. You must defer the caller to another officer or the public relations department for comment.

What do you do if a member of the public asks you a question you don't have an answer for?

It is natural that you will not know everything. As an entry level firefighter, it is important that you work hard to learn as much as you can about what you do and why you do it, but there is no expectation you know everything. It is appropriate to politely tell a member of the public that you have been assigned to do something for the safety of the public or other firefighters, and you will get your officer to give them a though answer as soon as they can.

Example: You have been assigned to vent a window on a home

that is full of smoke following a fire being put out. The homeowner comes up to you and states "Why are you going to break that window, the fire is out already". The best answer would be "we need to vent this window so that the smoke damage will be less, and the firefighters can finish up safely". If you were unsure, it would be inappropriate to make up an answer. It would be appropriate for you to say politely, my officer ordered me to vent this window for the safety of the firefighters inside, and for the protection of the structure. When he is available, I will ask him to come to you and explain in detail why we need to do this.

How do you reassure the member of the public in an emergency?

You should always wok to present yourself and the Department in a positive light. Dressing professionally and staying physically fit project an image of confidence and competence to the public. As a firefighter, you will meet many people in distress over your career. How you deal with people in difficult circumstances will define you as a firefighter. If you are confronted with a question scenario where it would seem appropriate to reassure a member of the public that is in distress, here are some tips:

1. Be honest. Don't tell somebody that everything will be alright, because it may not be. Instead, state "I am here for you." "I will do my best to help make things better". It is appropriate to state your confidence in your team and yourself. Be cautious about being overly familiar in using terms such as "sweetie" or "honey" with adults. Also, beware of minimizing the situation to try to make a person feel better. It is best to be supportive, professional, and human.

2. Keep in mind when dealing with children that firefighters with all their gear on can look scary. The SCBA mask can be intimidating. When speaking to a child, bend down to eye level, and, if safe, take off your mask so they can see your face.

You want to show empathy towards people in crisis vs. sympathy. Empathy is understanding what others are feeling because you have experienced it yourself or can put yourself in their shoes. Sympathy is acknowledging another person's difficulty by feeling bad for them. In this case, sympathy may be received as being patronizing to the person. It is not helpful to tell somebody "I know exactly how you feel, my aunt's house burned down last year". It would be more helpful to state "I am sorry for your loss, we are here for you. When the time is right, maybe it would be helpful to talk about how my family moved past a fire we recently experienced". In this case, you offer condolences, support, and an open-ended offer for conversation on how to get past the present difficulty.

How should an Entry level firefighter behave?

A. Be enthusiastic to learn and to work. Entry level firefighters can demonstrate leadership by being enthusiastic about learning how to use new equipment or implementing new procedures.

B. Show up early, stay late.

C. Upon arriving for your tour, talk to the outgoing shift. Learn about what has been going on in the firehouse.

D. Stay busy. Clean, organize, and study equipment and procedures.

E. Dress professionally and neatly. One way a probationary firefighter can demonstrate leadership is by dressing professionally and helping to set a tone of professionalism.

F. Find a good mentor. Look to find a senior firefighter who can show you the safe, correct way to do things. This person can also help you assimilate into the culture of the Department.

G. Be humble, yet confident in your duties.

H. Think about what your body language says. Keep your hands out of your pockets, and sit without slouching.

I. No one expects you to be the strongest or fastest. What is expected, is that you always give it your all, and keep coming back for more.

Part of the Human Relations component of the exam will present you with a set of stated rules and procedures. You will then be given a scenario and tasked with finding the best and worse course of action regarding the application of the rule. From a technical standing point, this will be testing your deductive reasoning skills.

Deductive Reasoning

Deduction is reasoned truth by a set of definitions. This may sound complex, but it is the fundamental basis for mathematics and a procedure everyone uses daily. Deductive reasoning begins with a general premise (or set of premises) and leads to a specific, rational conclusion via the application of logic. Deduction is the opposite of inductive reasoning, which derives broad generalizations from observed phenomena. Essentially, deductive reasoning applies a stated premise, or set of facts, to a group of things. When applied across members of a group, this type of truth statement is called a syllogism.

For example,

IF: A=B

AND: B=C

THUS: A=C

Successful deductive reasoning requires the ability to correctly identify members of a group without error; incorrect categorizations will lead to irrational conclusions. Furthermore, deductive reasoning relies upon the validity of the underlying premises (i.e. their "trueness" or "falseness") in addition to the application of logic. Therefore, the problem's starting point, its original agreed upon facts, must be correct. If the original premise(s) are erroneous, even if the logic used is sound, the result will still be incorrect.

Take for example, this general premise:

"Every octopus has eight arms."

A conditional statement is then posed as a problem:

"If this is an octopus, then it has eight arms."

It, therefore, logically follows:

"This is an octopus, so then it must have eight arms."

This is a sound deduction. The validity of the deduction, however, depends on the truth of the underlying premise. It remains true only as long as no seven armed octopuses are discovered. Additionally, this reasoning is not to be confused with the common logical error:

"This creature has eight arms, so it must be an octopus".

Not all eight armed creatures are octopuses, but all octopuses are eight armed creatures. The eight-armed creature could be a spider.

On the exam, you will be asked how to apply general rules to particular cases. There are two different types of deductive reasoning questions appearing on the firefighter exam:
1. Applying rules and procedures to situations
2. Applying definitions to the facts of situations

Applying Rules and Procedures:
In constructing firefighter exams, test makers treat department rules and procedures as general premises which must be applied situations. On the exam, deductive reasoning questions begin with a direct statement from the department. For example, a question could state the procedure for signing in before roll call. The question might then give a description of a firefighter arriving late to work. Then, the question will ask about how the firefighter should signing in.

When answering these questions, do not rely upon prior experience. You may be familiar with the policy or procedure being tested, but do not allow experience to cloud your reasoning. Everything you need to know to answer the question is contained in the procedure provided.

These questions often seem to present the greatest challenge to volunteer firefighters. Many volunteers have years of experience, specialized training, and are accustom to operating under a similar set of preexisting rules. Focus on the rules exactly as they are written. Answer the question from the perspective of a first day probationary firefighter.

Rules and procedures assure that protocol is enforced consistently, allow for a chain of command to operate, and enhance the ability of various agencies to coordinate a response to an emergency. These questions are designed to test your ability to follow and apply rules. There will not be any "trick" psychological questions in this part.

Here are some strategies for answering deductive reasoning questions:
1. Follow the steps in order.
2. Observe the conditional nature of the premise (when the rule is in effect).
3. Identify the negation of any procedure (when the rule is not in effect).
4. Recognize when there are exemptions to a rule, and know when to apply the exemption (the key words to help you identify exemptions are "unless", "except", "when", and "if").
5. If a premise has several parts, make sure the answer satisfies all the parts. When answering this type of question, reread the question and ask, "Is there anything missing from this answer?"
6. In choosing an answer, apply the rules exactly as written. Remember, this is an exam for an entry level position in

the department. The exam tests the degree to which you follow directions, not how well you interpret the merits of departmental protocol.

Here is a list of some standard operating procedures common to most professional fire departments. Use this list only as a guide to become familiar with rules. When taking the exam, rely only on the information provided in the question.

Confidentiality- Firefighters shall treat the official business of the department as confidential. Firefighters shall not release information concerning the name or condition of accident or crime victims.

Contact with the Public- Firefighters shall be courteous and civil when dealing with the public. Any conduct to the contrary shall not be tolerated.

Department Property- Firefighters shall be responsible for the good care of all property assigned to them and shall report to their commanding officer any loss, damage, or unserviceable condition of such property.

False Information- No firefighter shall complete any report using false or inaccurate information.

Gratuities- Firefighters shall not accept free admission for themselves or others to theaters or other places of amusements. Firefighters shall not receive money, gifts, gratuities, food/beverages, or ANY rewards as compensation for services rendered.

Identification- Firefighters shall give all proper information to persons requesting it in a careful, courteous and accurate manner. Firefighters shall give their names and badge numbers in a respectful manner to any person who may request the information.

Orders- Firefighters shall promptly obey any orders given by any officer of higher rank.

Statements- No member shall speak on behalf of the department unless authorized to do so by the fire commissioner.

Substance Use- Firefighters shall not consume any intoxicating liquors while on duty. Firefighters shall not take any medication, prescribed or otherwise, unless approved by the medical bureau.

Timeliness- Firefighters shall be punctual in reporting for duty at the time designated by the department.

Fire Prevention- All members of the department are responsible for the prevention of fires regardless of their duty assignment.

Uniform- Firefighters shall be in complete uniform when on duty. No mixture of civilian and uniform clothing shall be permitted in public or off-duty.

Applying Rules and Procedures

This exam requires the candidate to apply rules and procedures to situations. The test-taker is not expected to have any prior knowledge of the information. The rules are stated as part of the question. These questions resemble reading comprehension questions, but they are designed to test the candidate's ability to reason based on procedural stipulations. These questions define several different rules with oversimplified explanations. Answer this type of question based solely on the definition provided - **not from prior knowledge**.

After providing several definitions, the questions describe a specific situation. Pay careful attention to detail. Expect answer choices which are selected to trick a careless reader. Break definitions into segments; and then, make a mental checklist.

While reading, look for important punctuation marks like colons or semicolons that may be indicators of the separate parts of a definition. Also, watch out for the conjunctions "and" and "or". Use of the word "and", means that **two or more** parts must have occurred to fulfill the statement.

Strategies for Answering Deductive Reasoning Questions:

1. Read carefully. There are alluring false choices designed to fool careless readers.

2. Make sure your answer choice fulfills all parts of a given rule, policy, or definition.

3. Use only the information provided. Do not rely on your own knowledge of an actual rule or definition.

4. Keep in mind that these questions are meant to test your ability to follow directions. Your job is not to interpret the quality of a policy.

Sample Question: Applying Rules and Procedures

>**RULE:** Any fire apparatus should be inspected immediately prior to the start of each shift. Do not assume that a vehicle is in safe working condition. Check that all the lighting is operational, all emergency equipment is present, operate the siren, check engine, oil level, engine coolant level, gasoline level, tire pressure and condition, spare tire, lug wrench, jack, windshield wipers and windshield washer fluid level. Check the body of the vehicle for damaged or missing parts, and report any damaged or malfunctioning equipment to your lieutenant. At the end of your shift, leave the vehicle in safe operational condition for use by the next chauffer.
>
>**SITUATION:** Firefighter Davis is about to begin his shift when he discovers that his fire truck has a large scratch and dent in the right rear quarter panel. He knows that the vehicle did not have this dent yesterday, when he last drove it.

QUESTION: According to the rule, Davis should...

A. request a different vehicle

B. begin his shift, alert to any operating problems

C. find out which other officers have used the vehicle since his last shift

D. inform his lieutenant about the dented bumper

SOLUTION: Davis has discovered a dent in the quarter panel that did not exist when he last used it. The question asks what he should do about it. To answer the question, evaluate each of the choices.

Choice A The firefighter should NOT request a different vehicle. There is nothing in the rule that states that the firefighter should do this. Choice A is incorrect.

Choice B The firefighter should NOT begin his shift and be alert to any operating problems. The rule states that the firefighter should report any problems with the vehicle to his lieutenant. Choice B is incorrect.

Choice C The firefighter should NOT find out which other firefighters have used the vehicle since his last shift. There is nothing in the rule that states that firefighter should do this. Choice C is incorrect.

Choice D The firefighter should inform his lieutenant about the damaged quarter panel. This conforms to the given rule that states that the firefighter should report any problems, damage, or discrepancies to the lieutenant. Choice D is the correct answer.

Rule Relating to Leaves of Absence

1. Prepare a *leave of absence report* and it submit to the commanding officer for approval at least five days before leave commences, except in emergency.
2. Leaves may only be terminated at the discretion of the fire commissioner.
3. A member who is granted an extended leave of absence without pay must take all accrued leave prior to the start of the leave of absence, except for military leave.
4. Leave without pay for thirty (30) or more consecutive days during a year, except military leave, will reduce authorized vacation by 1/12 for each thirty (30) consecutive days of absence.
5. A member returning from leave without pay for one (1) year or more may not be granted un-accrued vacation until member performs active duty for a minimum of three (3) months, unless otherwise authorized by law.
6. A member of the service (uniformed or civilian) applying for any extended leave (e.g., educational leave with or without pay, hardship leave) is required to communicate with the Military and Extended Leave Desk for instructions.
7. Leave without pay may be granted to observe a religious holiday. No more than 1/6 of each battalion may be granted such leave.

Deductive Reasoning Questions:

1. If a firefighter has a documented family emergency and desires to apply for a leave of absence, what must he or she do?
A. wait five days; then submit the paperwork
B. go to his/her family and apply after the fact
C. submit paperwork immediately, thereby, requesting immediate leave
D. submit paperwork and wait the required 5 days

2. If a firefighter has been approved for a leave for educational purposes and an emergency strikes the community, who has the power to terminate *leaves of absence*?
A. the fire commissioner
B. each commanding officer
C. the mayor
D. No one. The leave was already granted.

3. If a member is called up for military service:
A. He must first use up all his accrued leave time.
B. He does not have to use his accrued leave time.
C. He must not go.
D. He must wait until a replacement is found.

4. A member goes on leave without pay for 31 days. She has accrued 12 vacation days. How many days will be deducted?
A. 12
B. 6
C. 3
D. 1

5. A member returns from a two-year leave of absence. How long must he or she wait until applying for a vacation?
A. immediately
B. 1 month
C. 3 months
D. 1 year

6. A member desires to take a leave of absence to attend law school. With whom must the member communicate?
A. lieutenant
B. commanding officer
C. internal investigations desk
D. Military and Extended Leaves Desk

7. A battalion has 60 members. The Easter religious holiday is approaching. How many members may be granted an unpaid leave of absence from the squad?
A. none
B. 6
C. 10
D. 60

Answers: (1. C, 2. A, 3. B, 4. D, 5. C, 6. D, 7. C)

Procedures for Utilizing the Information System

Purpose: to inform members of the requisite guidelines when accessing, creating, receiving, disclosing or otherwise maintaining an information system:

1. Access only those information systems which authorization has been granted, and under circumstances required, in the execution of duty.

2. Abide by any security terms/conditions associated with the information system, including those governing user passwords/logon procedures. All users must log out any time they leave the terminal.

3. Disclose information to others, including other firefighters, only as required in the execution of lawful duty.

4. Confirm identity and affiliation of the requestor of information and determine that release of information is lawful, prior to disclosure.

5. Maintain confidentiality of information when accessed, created, received, disclosed or otherwise maintained during course of duty.

Questions:

1. If a firefighter desires to use the information system, when is it permissible to borrow another firefighter's password?
A. during off-duty hours
B. during regular shift
C. Never because access is not authorized.
D. only with cooperating firefighter present

2. A firefighter is using the information system terminal and feels the urge to use the restroom. The firefighter should...
A. logoff
B. turn off screen
C. ask the lieutenant to watch the computer
D. Leave it on, since will take too long to reboot.

3. A firefighter has a friend who works for a local newspaper. The friend requests information from the firefighter. The firefighter should…
A. have the friend arrested
B. refer the friend to the office of media relations
C. allow the friend to only view the material, not print it
D. print the information requested

4. What should a firefighter do if someone calls on the house phone and states that they are with the FBI and needs information on a "crack house"?
A. offer to give the information
B. hang up
C. refer the caller to the commanding officer for verification of credentials
D. take down the caller's information and give the requested information

Answers: (1. C, 2. A, 3. B, 4. C)

Uniforms
1. Maintain at own expense articles prescribed for rank, position or duty. *Recruits wear uniform only after inspected and stamped by fire academy.*
2. Do not modify prescribed uniforms in any manner except as specifically authorized by higher authority.
3. Do not wear distinguishable items of the uniform with civilian clothes.
4. Do not wear uniform, shield or display IDENTIFICATION CARD while participating in a rally, demonstration or other public assemblage except as authorized by the department.
5. Wear the uniform of the day. Commanding officers or unit commanders may authorize a specialized uniform only after requesting and receiving approval from the Fire Commissioner's Uniform and Equipment Review Committee. Submit requests to the Office of the Chief of Department: Attn: Uniform and Equipment Sub-Committee.
Wear the uniform when directed, if assigned to light duty or to duty in civilian clothes.
6. While performing duty indoors, in uniform, wear regulation seasonal shirt and trousers.
7. Wear the prescribed uniform, if regularly assigned to duty in uniform, when appearing at a hearing, or at the office of a ranking officer above the rank of captain, except if off duty, on sick report, or if excused by competent authority.
8. Purchase regulation caps, bunker gear and all items of uniform which are sewn or attached to the uniform, from the equipment section or other authorized supplier.
9. Necessary uniform changes, other than those listed in Step 1 will be made as directed by the lieutenant commander/counterpart:
   a. The lieutenant commander/counterpart shall authorize the removal, if desired, of the duty jacket/summer blouse whenever the temperature for a **specific** tour is expected to rise above 65 degrees

Fahrenheit.

b. The lieutenant commander/counterpart shall authorize the wearing of the **optional** short sleeve shirt whenever the temperature for a **specific** tour is expected to rise above 70 degrees Fahrenheit.

Questions:

1. A firefighter desires to replace uniform articles. He or she must…
A. submit a voucher for payment from the department
B. request the new articles from the quartermaster.
C. pay for the articles from an authorized vendor
D. wait until the annual uniform fund is established

2. A firefighter desires to place a small gold cross on the left collar of the uniform. Who may authorize such an alteration?
A. the Commissioner's Uniform and Equipment Review Committee
B. the union
C. the firefighter's clergy
D. fellow firefighters

3. A firefighter desires to attend an immigration rally. She/he must…
A. wear "class A" uniform
B. not wear their shield or ID card
C. not attend any rally
D. may proudly display his/her badge if Class A uniform is worn

4. When appearing at a hearing, firefighters should wear:
A. street clothes
B. regular uniform
C. suit and tie for men, dress and blouse for ladies
D. former military uniform, if ever in service

5. From whom may a firefighter purchase a cap?
A. any sporting goods store
B. from an authorized retailer
C. from fire academy
D. from a retired firefighter

6. The temperature is expected to rise to 68 degrees Fahrenheit for a specific tour. The lieutenant may authorize:
A. shorts
B. removal of duty jacket or summer blouse
C. street clothes
D. sneakers, socks, and athletic wear

7. The temperature is expected to rise to 80 degrees Fahrenheit. The lieutenant may authorize the use of…
A. shorts
B. short- sleeved shirt
C. sneakers
D. street clothes

Answers: (1. C, 2. A, 3. B, 4. B, 5. B, 6. B, 7. B)

Rule

The Counterterrorism Bureau recently distributed personal protective equipment to over 30,000 uniformed members of the fire department. This equipment is designed to enhance the personal safety of uniformed members in the event of a disaster or catastrophic incident, including those of a chemical or biological nature. Included in the personal protective kit is a tactical response hood contained in a cloth carry pouch. This item is designed to be attached to the belt worn by uniformed members. As such, it should be carried by, and available to, all uniformed members on duty.

I. Members are reminded that the tactical response hood is designed for a single escape of up to 15 minutes from a contaminated area. Hoods do not provide oxygen and are not intended for use in an oxygen-deprived environment.

II. Therefore, effective immediately, uniformed members of the service will carry the tactical response hood as follows:
    a. Members performing fire inspection duties in a department vehicle will have the hood and pouch available in the vehicle;
    b. Members performing foot fire inspection duties will carry the tactical response hood by attaching the pouch to their belts on the side opposite which the member carries his/her walkie talkie;
    c. Members performing administrative or other duties inside a department facility will have the tactical response hood and pouch readily available at all times.

III. The balance of the personal protective equipment issued to uniformed members of the department will be carried in department vehicles by those members operating such vehicles. All other uniformed members will have the balance of the personal protective equipment readily available (i.e. stored in a department locker).

IV. Any provisions of the Department Manual or other department directive in conflict with the contents of this order are suspended.

Questions:

1. A firefighter is on fire inspection in a department vehicle, she should:
A. wear the personal protective equipment
B. carry the personal protective equipment on her belt on the opposite side from her walkie talkie.
C. give the personal protective equipment to family
D. leave the personal protective equipment in the trunk of the vehicle

2. In the event of a chemical attack, the hood is designed to protect a firefighter
A. for a shift
B. for 15 minutes
C. for 1 hour
D. indefinitely

3. A firefighter is assigned to foot fire inspection. Where should the firefighter keep the personal protective gear?
A. in a backpack
B. in the firehouse
C. at the command post
D. on a belt

4. A member is assigned to light duty at the battalion following an accident while on duty. The firefighter…
A. must wear their personal protective device on his/her belt
B. must keep the personal protective device in her/his locker
C. does not need the personal protective device
D. must keep the personal protective device close at hand

Answers: (1. B, 2. B, 3. D, 4. D)

Human Relations Practice Question Set

EXAMPLE:

1. While on duty, you overhear a conversation between two firefighters. One of them is making inappropriate comments about the condition of a deceased victim from a recent fire. The comments also included racial overtones. What would you do?

   A. Ignore the comments and carry on with your work. Gallows humor is part of fire department culture.
   B. Join in with the comments, but keep the comments clean.
   C. Immediately challenge the inappropriate behavior, and explain how the comments are not in line with department policy.
   D. Report the comments to the lieutenant. It is their responsibility to deal with this kind of issue.

The correct answer to this question is:

   C. Immediately challenge the inappropriate behavior and explain how the comments are not in line with department policy. No bullying, harassment or inappropriate comments are tolerated in the fire department. It is everybody's responsibility to challenge them.

2. A member of your company left training to take an important personal phone call. While he was out, he missed some important information regarding a change to specific rescue procedures. What would you do?

   A. Immediately explain to him what he missed and check that he understands.
   B. Inform your lieutenant of his absence so that he can tell him what he missed.
   C. Do nothing. He will probably find out about the changes through other work colleagues.
   D. Inform the member that he missed critical information, and that he needed to confer with the officer about what was missed.

3. While working at the scene of a construction accident, you notice a firefighter from another company using an item of equipment that you do not recognize. What would you do?

   A. Tell the firefighter to stop using the equipment since everybody was not trained on it. The new equipment was not issued to you, so you have no responsibility to know how to use it.
   B. Approach the firefighter and ask if you can try the equipment. It would be a good idea to start using the equipment, so that you become familiar with it. Good firefighters are always learning.
   C. Wait until you get back to the firehouse, and ask your officer if you can contact battalion and request to be trained on the equipment.
   D. Wait until getting back to the station, then get a colleague to show you how to use it.

4. Firefighters are often required to enter people's homes in order to test for gas leaks.

While at a home to test a gas leak, a resident offers you a reward of $100 as a thank you for finding an extinguished pilot light. What would you do?

   A. Thank them for the money, and split it with your company.
   B. Thank them for the money, take it home, and give it to the burn unit as a donation.
   C. Thank them for their kind offer, but explain that you are unable to accept gifts or gratuities.
   D. Tell them "No, that is bribery" sternly and clearly, so that everyone present can hear.

5. During a fire, the captain gives you instructions to immediately stop what you are doing and call in more companies via the dispatcher, due to the fire spreading. Once you have received the instructions, what would you do?

   A. Finish off the job that you are doing before contacting the dispatcher to request more resources.
   B. Immediately stop what you are doing, if safe to do so, before contacting the dispatcher to request more resources. Once you have requested the resources and confirmed that the dispatcher fully understands your request, you will then inform the captain that the message has been sent. You would then return to the previous task.
   C. Because you are already involved in another task, pass the message onto another firefighter so that he can request the resources. Team work is an important aspect of the job.
   D. Immediately stop what you are doing, if safe to do so, before contacting the dispatcher to request more resources. Once you have requested the resources, and confirmed that the dispatcher fully understands your request, you will then go back to what you were doing.

6. While fighting a fire in an attached row of two story apartments, which of the following tasks would you carry out first?

   A. Check your equipment before using it, so that it is safe.
   B. Fight the fire.
   C. Evacuate the people inside the burning building.
   D. Contact the dispatcher and ask for more resources.

7. While working a motor vehicle accident involving four people trapped inside a car, which of the following tasks would you carry out last?

   A. Make sure the car is safe and stable before working on it.
   B. Carry out an immediate assessment of all the casualties in the car to ascertain their injuries and make sure they are breathing.
   C. Get the Hurst tool ready to extricate the casualties.
   D. Complete the injury report.

8. You are working a fire inside a house, searching for casualties. When you entered the building you had 45 minutes of air in your cylinder. It has been 35 minutes, and you are breathing heavily due to exertion. What should you do?

   A. check the gauge
   B. slow down your breathing
   C. split breathing between the mask and the room air
   D. wait until the air begins to be restricted

9. During a fire safety visit to a local school, you notice that a number of the fire doors are wedged open illegally. What do you do?

   A. Ignore it for the time being. That is not why you are there.
   B. Report the situation to your battalion chief, when you return to the firehouse.
   C. Pull the fire alarm to immediately evacuate the school.
   D. Inform the school custodian that he/she must remove the wedges immediately, and explain that the fire doors must not be wedged open. In addition, you inform your supervising officer.

10. You are working an incident that involves a fire in a warehouse. You notice that the fire is starting to spread to a neighboring building. What would you do?

    A. Quickly run over to where the fire is spreading and shout for help.
    B. Stay calm, carry out an assessment of the situation, write down what you see, passing the details on to your officer, so he can decide what to do next.
    C. Immediately inform the officer of the situation, then tackle the fire preventing further spread in line with operational procedures.
    D. Inform the officer, and then wait for back up to arrive before taking any action.

11. While off-duty you are attending a movie in a crowded theatre. You notice that a small fire has begun in the front row of the theatre. What do you do?

    A. Yell "FIRE!" and begin moving people to the back of the theatre.
    B. Calmly go to the usher and inform him of the fire, pull the alarm, then ensure 911 has been called.
    C. Get a water can from the lobby, and put out the fire.
    D. Leave quickly without telling anybody.

12. You are called to a fire in a factory. As you turn the corner in the fire engine, you notice a gang of youths running away. You suspect that they may have started the fire deliberately. What would you do?

   A. Any issues relating to who started the fire are not your concern. You are there to fight the fire.
   B. Suggest to the captain that half of the team tackle the fire, while the other half run after the youths.
   C. Make a mental note of the description of the youth. Fight the fire, and call the police. The police can investigate the cause of the fire.
   D. Put the fire out first, and then drive around in the fire engine looking for the youths.

Answer questions 13-15 based on the following passage:

With water safety operations, there is an excellent example of how a rescuer can prioritize a rescue response to help assist a struggling victim while maximizing the rescuer's safety.

REACH – THROW – ROW – GO is the classic model.

REACH:

Victim(s) are located close to the shoreline and the rescuer(s) can retrieve them by reaching with their persons, rescue pole or hook, an oar, or a backboard without having to enter the water. Victim(s) must be conscious, alert, and able to grab and hold on to the reaching device for this method to be considered.

THROW:

Victim(s) are too far away from the shoreline to be reached with a rigid object. Rescuers can throw ropes, rope bags, flotation rings or discs tied to a rope, a PFD tied to a rope to retrieve the victim without having to enter the water. Victim(s) must be conscious, alert, and able to grab and hold on to the thrown object for this method to be considered.

ROW:

Victim(s) are too far away from the shoreline to be reached or to have a flotation device thrown to them. Rescuers must use a boat or approved watercraft to access and retrieve the victim(s) without having to enter the water. Once close enough to the victim(s), rescuers can reach, throw, or lift them directly into the boat (whichever method is easiest and safest). Victim(s) may be conscious and alert or unconscious.

GO:

Rescuers must physically enter the water and swim to the victim(s) to retrieve them. This method may be used from the shoreline or from a boat depending on the circumstances. This method is typically used for unconscious victims but may also be used for conscious and alert victims that are in distress or unable to grab and hold on to a flotation device. Only those rescuers, who are strong swimmers, should enter the water to retrieve a victim.

13. Your company has been called to the scene of a drowning, and you notice a child struggling to stay afloat. What would you do?

- A. You would take your clothes off to prevent from sinking and swim in after the boy. You are a strong swimmer, and would be able to rescue him.
- B. You would reach out to the victim with a hook. Then try to pull him to the side with the help of the company.
- C. You would take your clothes off and go into the water up to waste height with a rope securely tied around your waste. This way you would be able to rescue him without placing yourself in any danger.
- D. You are not permitted to enter the water without a buoyancy aid; therefore, you are powerless to help the boy.

14. You come to the scene of a swimmer in distress. The swimmer is struggling but is too far out for you to reach with a hook. What would you do?

   A. row out a small boat
   B. swim out
   C. throw a line
   D. wait for the marine unit

15. You come to the scene of a swimmer in distress. The swimmer is struggling but is too far out for you to reach with a rescue line. What would you do?

   A. row out a small boat
   B. swim out
   C. throw a line
   D. wait for the marine unit

16. A firefighter colleague, who is from a different religion than yourself, asks you if you would cover his tour, so he may celebrate a holiday. What would you do?

   A. This has nothing to do with work, and therefore, he should not be allowed time off. You would not cover the shift.
   B. You would refuse.
   C. You would be happy to cover part of the tour, if he promised to pay back the time later.
   D. You would be happy to cover part of the shift if the officer in charge approves the change.

Base you answer to questions 17-20 on the following statement:

In first aid scenarios, the first thing learned is to survey the scene for safety. Oftentimes, a first responder is injured because they rush into a dangerous situation. Use the 5 senses. Listen for clues to the danger, and use the sense of smell to check for gas or other fumes. Look for wires or other dangers. Once the scene is deemed safe, then check the victim. The first thing we check for on a victim is the pulse. Then we assess consciousness and conduct a secondary assessment for further injury. Assessment begins with most critical functions and moves to less critical things such as cuts and abrasions.

17. You come to the scene of a motor vehicle accident involving a child apparently struck by a car. What would you do first?

    A. survey the scene
    B. conduct a secondary assessment
    C. check for a pulse
    D. find the driver

18. You come to the scene of a motor vehicle accident involving a child apparently struck by a car. What would you do second?

    A. survey the scene
    B. conduct a secondary assessment
    C. check to see if the child has a pulse
    D. find the driver

19. You come to the scene of a motor vehicle accident involving a child apparently struck by a car. What would you do third?

    A. survey the scene
    B. conduct a secondary assessment
    C. check for a pulse
    D. find the driver

20. After surveying the scene of an electrocution victim and determining that that the power is off, what would you do next?

    A. begin chest compressions
    B. transport the victim
    C. assess if the victim is conscious and has a pulse
    D. begin mouth to mouth

21. A member of the public walks into the firehouse and asks for the deadline to file for an inspection. You do not know the answer. The best way to respond to this request is?
A. Tell the person what you think the answer might be.
B. Refer the person to your supervisor.
C. Say that you are not allowed to give out that information to the public.
D. Inform the person that you don't know but will find out.

22. If a firefighter is unable to do what a citizen asks, the firefighter should avoid:
A. Quoting organizational policy regarding the citizen's request.
B. Explaining why it cannot be done.
C. Making specific statements.
D. Offering alternatives.

23. Of the following, which would be the least frustrating for a citizen to hear from a firefighter?
A. You will have to…
B. I will do my best.
C. Let me see what I can do.
D. He/She should be back any minute.

24. When dealing with members of the public, a firefighter's apologies, if necessary, should not be:
A. immediate
B. official
C. sincere
D. personal

25. The ability to provide the promised service or product dependably and accurately may be defined as:
A. assurance
B. responsiveness
C. courtesy
D. reliability

26. To be most useful to a department, feedback received from residents should be each of the following except:
A. centered on feedback from other government employees
B. ongoing
C. focused on a limited number of indicators
D. available to every employee in the organization

27. Once a human relations problem is identified, each of the following should become a part of the resolution process except:
A. following up on the problem resolution
B. making whatever promises are necessary
C. providing the member of the public with what was originally requested
D. listening and responding to every complaint given by the resident

28. To arrive at a fair solution to a service problem, one should first:
A. defend the organization
B. ask questions to understand and confirm the nature of the problem
C. listen to the resident's description of the problem
D. determine and implement a solution to the problem

29. A firefighter strives to be prompt when addressing customer complaints. Which service factor is the firefighter demonstrating?
A. Assurance
B. Responsiveness
C. Empathy
D. Reliability

30. Firefighters will achieve the best results if they strive to represent
A. the entire organization
B. the resident
C. the department
D. their supervisor

31. A person approaches you and tells you of many complaints he has about your department. You should first:
A. Assume that he is just blowing off steam and ignore the criticisms.
B. Check into the legitimacy of the complaints.
C. Ask for advice from your supervisor on the best way to handle the person.
D. Regard the complaints as accurate and take immediate steps to correct them.

32. When a resident presents a firefighter with a request, the firefighter's **first** reaction should *usually* be a(n):
A. Apology
B. Friendly greeting
C. Statement of organizational policy regarding the request.
D. Request for clarifying information.

33. A member of the public appears to be mildly irritated when lodging a complaint. It is most appropriate for a firefighter to demonstrate _____ in reaction to the complaint.
A. urgency
B. empathy
C. nonchalance
D. surprise

34. If a firefighter is aware that the organization is not capable of meeting a resident's expectations, the firefighter's first responsibility would be to:
A. tell the customer of the organization's inability to comply.
B. shape the customer's expectations to match what the organization can do for him/her.
C. encourage the customer to believe that the organization can do as he/she asks.
D. refer the customer to a higher level for further communication.

35. According to most members of the public, _____ prevents good listening on the part of a firefighter when a resident is speaking.
A. technological devices (telephones, pagers, walkie-talkies)
B. frequent interruptions by other staff or residents
C. asking unnecessary questions
D. background noise

36. Instead of directly saying no to a resident, firefighters will usually get the best results with a reply that begins with the words:
A. I'll try
B. I don't believe
C. You can
D. It's not our policy

37. A resident appears to be mildly irritated when lodging a complaint. The most appropriate action for a firefighter to take while attempting resolution is to:
A. allow venting of frustrations
B. enlist the resident in generating solutions
C. show emotional neutrality
D. create calm

38. When listening to a citizen during a face-to-face meeting, the most appropriate physical presentation is:
A. crossed arms
B. frowning
C. leaning towards the resident
D. staring at a spot over the resident's shoulder

39. Most what is communicated during face-to-face meetings is conveyed by
A. word choices
B. body language
C. verbal tone
D. clothing

40. When a citizen submits a written complaint, the firefighter should select a response that avoids
A. addressing every allegation in the written complaint
B. a personal tone
C. a pre-formulated response
D. a proposed solution or remedy

Human Relations Practice Question Answer Key
2. D
3. C
4. C
5. B
6. A
7. D
8. A
9. D
10. C
11. B
12. C
13. B
14. C
15. A
16. D
17. A
18. C
19. B
20. C

21. D. It is always best to be honest and admit that you do not know the answer but will attempt to find out. It is never a good idea to guess an answer as it may result in inaccurate information. Referring the resident to someone else is not ideal. If someone else in the firehouse knows the answer than you should ask them directly and increase your own knowledge to better serve the next resident.

22. A. It is always better to explain the reasoning behind policies and offer alternatives than to merely quote an established policy. For many residents, this can be a source of frustration as it still leaves their needs unmet and many questions on how to resolve their issue.

23. C. This response tells a resident that the firefighter will make every effort to satisfy a request or to offer alternatives.

24. B. Official apologies should come from a supervisor or higher-level of authority within the organization. Not only does this reduce the pressure on the firefighter to bear the full responsibility of a situation, but it provides a level of authority to the apology (if necessary).

25. D. Reliability is defined as consistency and accuracy in judgment or results.

26. A. Feedback from other government employees overlooks what usually represents the largest customer base of a fire department (members of the public) and presents often biased and skewed feedback.

27. B. Promises that cannot be delivered on can cause additional complaints and issues with the public and should be avoided at all costs.

28. C. Listening to a citizen's description of the problem in its entirety is the first step in the process. Once you have heard the description you should ask clarifying questions to better understand the nature of the problem.

29. B. Responsiveness is defined as readily reacting.

30. A. By representing the entire organization, the firefighter will achieve results that are consistent with the entire organization's goals, will minimize changes that unduly negatively impact divisions or departments of the organization, while satisfying the needs of the public.

31. B. The first step to take is to determine how valid the individual's complaints are. Then, you can decide whether further action is needed or the complaints were unfounded and require no further action.

32. D. To best satisfy an individual's request, it is vital to know as many details of the request as possible and remove any uncertainties that could result in duplicating work or increasing the resident's distress.

33. A. A quick and motivated effort to resolve a complaint is the most effective way to prevent a mild irritation to escalating to a more serious problem. While empathy is valuable it does not resolve a complaint and nonchalance or surprise can further escalate a situation by appearing indifferent or even antagonistic.

34. B. Firefighters are in the unique position in that their interaction with a member of the public can influence an individual's expectations. By laying the framework for what the organization can accomplish and setting reasonable expectations the resident's level of satisfaction with the result can be increased.

35. B. When a firefighter does not focus on the customer and instead interrupts their interaction to address other individuals it is perceived that the firefighter has not heard what the resident is saying, is not paying attention to the issue, and does not care about the issue.

36. C. Of all the choices, only C provides an action for the member of the public, a source of potential relief. The other choices imply directly and indirectly that relief is either not possible or not likely, which can be highly discouraging and frustrating.

37. B. By enlisting the resident in providing solutions the

representative can get a feel for the result that the resident is looking for and ultimately what will resolve their complaint. While not all the alternatives presented by a member of the public may be feasible it can provide a starting point for realistic resolutions that can meet the same goal.

38. C. Leaning towards a person during a conversation is a nonverbal cue that expresses interest and attention.

39. B. Over 50% of what we perceive in a face-to-face discussion is expressed through our body language, how we stand, our facial expressions, our arm gestures etc.

40. C. Pre-formulated responses can be impersonal or overly generic and give the impression that issues are commonplace and have not been successfully responded to. A more personalized approach that is slightly less formal and addresses the specific nature of the complaint, including remedies to the issue is preferred and more effective.

Mechanical Ability

Mechanical ability or aptitude is the capacity to apply general physical principles to solve specific mechanical problems. In other words, it describes a person's ability to understand the way in which objects work and move. The concept of mechanical aptitude includes several components: general mechanical reasoning, visual/spatial relations, and specific tool knowledge.

Mechanical reasoning is the understanding of the ways in which simple machines work.

Simple machines are defined as those requiring the application of a single force to achieve a work outcome. Some examples of simple machines are the wheel and axle, lever, and inclined plane.

Visual/spatial relations refer to the orientation and movement of objects in different directions (i.e. angles) while still maintaining those objects original characteristics.

Tool knowledge refers to specific familiarity with common tools and the ways they are used. It is sometimes thought to be separate from mechanical aptitude, because it is built upon fundamental mechanical reasoning and visual/spatial abilities.

Levers

The simplest machine, and perhaps the most familiar, is the lever. A seesaw is an example of a lever in which one weight balances the other. All levers have three basic parts: the fulcrum (F), a force or effort (E), and a resistance (R).

Look at the lever in figure 1-1. The parts are: the pivotal point (fulcrum) (F); the effort (E), which is applied at a distance (A) from the fulcrum; and a resistance (R), which acts at a distance (A) from the fulcrum. Distances A and G are the arms of the lever.

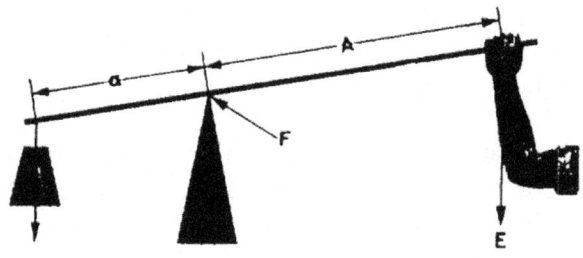

Classes of Levers

The location of the fulcrum (the fixed pivotal point) in relation to the resistance (weight) and the effort determines the lever class. Levers differ primarily in the relative points where effort is applied, resistance is overcome, and the fulcrum's location.

First Class

In first class levers the fulcrum is located between the effort and the resistance. First class levers have the effort and the resistance on opposite sides of the fulcrum, and effort and resistance move in opposite directions. The seesaw is a good example of a first-class lever. The amount of weight and the distance from the fulcrum can be varied to suit the need. Crowbars, shears, and pliers are all examples of first class levers.

Second Class

The second class of lever has the fulcrum at one end, the effort applied at the other end, and the resistance somewhere between those points. The wheelbarrow is a good example of a second-class lever. If 50 pounds of effort is applied to the handles of a wheelbarrow 4 feet from the fulcrum (wheel), 200 pounds of weight can be lifted 1 foot from the fulcrum. Levers of the first and second class are commonly used to help in overcoming big resistances with a relatively small effort.

Third Class

Sometimes speeding up the movement of resistance is desired, although it requires the use of a large amount of effort. Levers that accomplish this outcome are class three levers. Third class levers are made when force is applied between the fulcrum and the resistance. The human arm is an example a third-class lever. This lever action makes it possible for quick flexion of the arms. The elbow is the fulcrum, and, the bicep muscle, which ties onto the forearm about an inch below the elbow, applies the effort. The hand is the resistance. In the split second it takes the biceps muscle to contract an inch, the hand has moved through the air in a much larger arc.

Referring to the lever diagram, it takes a big pull at **E** to overcome a relatively small resistance at **R**. To experience this principle, try closing a door by pushing on it about 3 or 4 inches from the hinges (fulcrum).

Important Points:

- The fulcrum can be moved depending on the weight of the load to be lifted or the desired force exerted.
- The closer the load is to the fulcrum, the easier it is to move.
- The shorter side of a lever has more work to do to counter the effect of a longer side.
- Whenever force is applied to a point more distant from the fulcrum, less force is needed to accomplish the same amount of work (i.e. more leverage is added). Hence, an equal amount of force will do more work as it moves away from the fulcrum.

Tips for Answering Lever Questions:

- Evaluate the relative weights of the load(s) on the lever.
- Assess the distance between the load from the fulcrum and the force from the fulcrum.

MECHANICAL ADVANTAGE

Since first and second class levers can be used to magnify the applied force, they provide a positive mechanical advantage. The third-class lever provides a fractional mechanical advantage, which is really a mechanical disadvantage—more force is required than the load to be lifted.

The six classic simple machines are the lever, wedge, wheel and axle, inclined plane, screw, and the pulley.

Pulleys

A pulley is a wheel that has a length of rope wrapped around it and turns by the action of the rope in the groove. There are different types of pulleys. Pulleys are either fixed or movable. Fixed pulleys are attached at one place. The fixed pulley helps make work easier by changing the direction of the effort.

- With a single pulley, pulling down on the rope can lift an object attached to the other end. The single pulley is used in flagpoles, cranes, and water wells.
- Movable pulleys are attached to objects being lifted. As the rope is pulled, the object and the pulley move together. This pulley does not change the direction of the effort, but it does multiply the effort. Using fixed and movable pulleys together can result in a large mechanical advantage.
- Multiple pulleys can work together to move objects horizontally (such as on the conveyor belt at a grocery store) or distribute loads to allow the same amount of force (input) to do more work.
- Two pulleys of the same size that are connected by a moving belt turn at the same speed and in the same direction. If there is a twist in the belt, the pulleys will move in opposite directions.
- When moving at the same speed, smaller pulleys make more revolutions in the same amount of time as larger pulleys.

Block and Tackle

Usually used to lift heavy loads, block and tackle is a system of two or more pulleys with a rope threaded between them. The pulleys are assembled together to form blocks and then those blocks are paired so that one is fixed and one moves with the load. Rope is threaded through the pulleys to a provide mechanical advantage which amplifies the force applied to the rope.

Wheel and Axle

The wheel-and-axle machine consists of a wheel (sometimes crank) rigidly attached to an axle. A doorknob, steering wheel, and lug wrench are all examples of a wheel-and-axle. Each of these devices use the wheel-and-axle to multiply the force exerted.

The front wheel of an automobile is not a wheel-and-axle machine because the axle does not turn with the wheel.

The wheel and axle can be used to speed up motion. The rear wheel sprocket of a bike, along with the rear wheel itself, are both examples of this simple machine. When pedaling, the sprocket is attached to the wheel; so, the combination is a true wheel and axle machine.

Assume that the sprocket has a circumference of 6 inches, and the wheel circumference is 60 inches. If the sprocket is turned at a rate of one revolution per second, each sprocket tooth moves at a speed of 6 inches per second. Since the wheel makes one revolution for each revolution made by the sprocket, the tire must move a distance of 60 inches per second. So, for every 6-inch movement of a point on the sprocket, a corresponding point on the wheel has moved 60 inches.

Since a complete revolution of the sprocket and wheel requires only 1 second, the speed of the wheel is 60 inches per second (10 times the speed of a tooth on the sprocket).

NOTE: Both sprocket and wheel make the same number of revolutions per second, so the speed of turning is the same.

The force applied to a lever turns it around a fulcrum. The sheave on a fall starts to rotate the sheave of the block. Similarly, when turning the steering wheel of a car, it starts to rotate the steering column.

Effort on the lever arm or the rim of the wheel causes it to rotate about the axle in one direction. If the rotation occurs in the same direction as the hands of a clock, then that direction clockwise. If the rotation occurs in the opposite direction from that of the hands of a clock, that direction of rotation is counterclockwise.

A glance at figure 3-3 will make clear the meaning of these terms.

The force acting on the handle of a carpenter's brace depends not only on the amount of that force, but also on the distance from the handle to the center of rotation.

This is known as a moment of force, or torque (pronounced *tork*). When two equal forces at equal distances on opposite sides of a fulcrum are applied, and move in opposite directions, they cause rotation about the fulcrum.

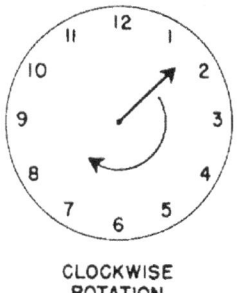

CLOCKWISE
ROTATION

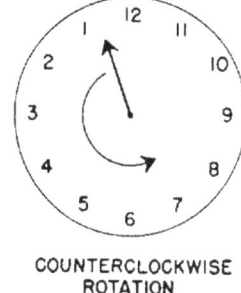

COUNTERCLOCKWISE
ROTATION

Inclined Plane, Wedge, and Screw

Inclined Plane

When raising a load, the inclined plane overcomes a large resistance by applying a small force over a longer distance. Examples of inclined planes include ramps and mountain roads. The mechanical advantage of an inclined plane is equal to the length of the plane divided by the height. Therefore, a ramp 10 feet long at height of 5 feet has a mechanical advantage of 2.

Wedge

The wedge is a specific application of the inclined plane. The wedge is two inclined planes set base to base. Long, slim wedges provide a high degree of mechanical advantage. Blades of knives, axes, hatchets, and chisels act as wedges. When driving the wedge full-length into the material to be split, the material is forced apart an equal distance to the width of the wedge's broad end.

Screw

The screw is a modification of the inclined plane into spiral form. Geometrically, the screw is an inclined plane wrapped around a cylinder. As in all machines, the mechanical advantage equals the resistance divided by the effort. Making use of the large amounts of friction, large amounts of circular motion are converted into very small amounts of straight line motion.

For an illustration, cut a sheet of paper in the shape of a right triangle and an inclined plane is formed. Wind this paper around a pencil. As the pencil is turned, the paper is wound so that its' hypotenuse forms a spiral thread. The pitch of the screw and paper is the distance between identical points on the same threads measured along the length of the screw.

Key Points:

- Load and force move in the same direction along a plane. When upward force is applied to push a load up a plane, the load also moves upward. When downward force is applied to push a load down a plane, the load also moves downward.

- Objects moving along an inclined plane will travel across a longer distance over a longer period than if lifted directly up or dropped straight down.

- When moving an object up an incline, gravity is pulling the object downward. Thus, the force needed to move an object up an incline is greater than the effort needed to move an object down an incline.

- Friction is created where the surface of an object meets the surface of an inclined plane. This resistance makes the work of moving the object more difficult whether moving the object up or down the plane.

- The steeper an inclined plane, the more easily an object moves down it. The opposite is also true: the steeper the plane, the more difficult it is to move an object up it.

- Force and load move in different directions. Consider the force to swing an ax downward, the load (wood) breaks apart and falls to the sides.

- The more resistance that a wedge encounters, the greater the force that will be needed to accomplish the work.

- The turning direction (clockwise or counterclockwise) dictates whether the hold between a screw and other object is tightened or loosened. If being tightened, each consecutive rotation of the screw will move it further into the object and make the hold stronger. If being loosened, each rotation of the screw will make the hold weaker.

- Standard threading requires clockwise (right) rotation to tighten and counterclockwise
(left) rotation to loosen the hold. The colloquial phrase "righty-tighty, lefty-loosey" can help you remember this rule. ***Some screws have a reverse thread, in which case the opposite is true. Unless otherwise specified, you should use the rule of standard threading to answer questions.***

- The distance between the threads depends on the slope of the inclined plane – the steeper the slope, the wider the thread. Screws with less distance between the threads are easier to turn.

Tips for Answering Inclined Plane, Wedge, and Screw Questions:

- Evaluate the components (e.g., weight, size, and material) of the load(s) on the plane.
- Assess the angle of the incline in relation to gravity and/or other inclines presented in the question.
- Consider the effect of gravity and resistance.
- Evaluate the angle of the wedge to determine the relative force needed to accomplish the work.
- Determine whether standard threading or reverse threading applies.
- Evaluate the direction in which force is being applied.
- If being asked which of two screws will be more easily inserted into an object, determine which has the most distance between threads.

Gears

A gear (or cogwheel) is a rotating machine with cut teeth, or cogs, which mesh with another toothed part to transmit torque. Two or more gears working in a sequence are called a gear train or, in many cases, a transmission. Such gear arrangements produce a mechanical advantage through a gear ratio, and thus, they are considered simple machines. Geared devices can change the speed, torque, and direction of a power source. One advantage of gears is the lack of slippage. For example, there is usually a creep or slippage in a belt drive. However, since gear teeth are always in mesh, there is not any slippage of the belt.

An eggbeater provides a simple demonstration of the three jobs that gears accomplish. They can change the direction of motion, increase (or decrease) the speed of an applied motion, and magnify (or reduce) the applied force. Gears also provide positive drive.

In the following example, see the diagram below.

The crank handle turns in the direction shown by the arrow—clockwise—when viewed from the right. The 32 teeth on the large vertical wheel (A) mesh with the 8 teeth on the right-hand horizontal wheel (B), which rotates as shown by the arrow. Notice that as B turns in a clockwise direction, its' teeth mesh with those of wheel C and cause wheel C to revolve in the opposite direction.

The rotation of the crank handle has been transmitted by gears to the beater blades, which also rotate. Now figure out how the gears change the speed of motion. There are 32 teeth on gear A and 8 teeth on gear B. However, the gears mesh, so that one complete revolution of A results in four complete revolutions of gear B. And since gears B and C have the same number of teeth, one revolution of B results in one revolution of C. Thus, the blades revolve four times as fast as the crank handle. The force required to turn the handle is greater than the force applied to the frosting by the blades. This results in a mechanical advantage of less than one.

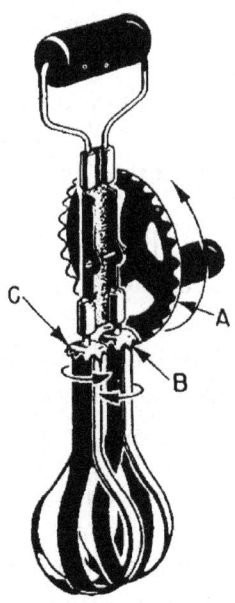

Tips for Answering Gear Questions:

- Choose a gear with a known direction of movement as a starting point (called the driving gear because it dictates the direction the other gears will move). Follow the movement of the driving gear to the point of contact with the next gear in the series.

- Focusing on this contact point (where force is applied), determine the direction the next gear in the series will rotate. To do this, ask which direction the teeth of the driving gear will move the teeth of the other gear.

- If the gear in question is not in direct contact with the driving gear, repeat the steps above to determine the direction that each gear will move until you reach the gear identified in the question.

- When there are several gears in a series, one helpful technique is to draw arrows on each gear to keep track of each rotation in the series.

- When the teeth of two gears fit together and one gear turns, it will cause the other gear to turn, but in the opposite direction.

- When the gears are the same size and they have the same number of teeth, they both turn at the same speed.
- When moving at the same speed, smaller gears make more revolutions in the same amount of time as larger gears.

Work

Work (in the mechanical sense) is accomplished when a resistance is overcome by a force acting through a measurable distance. Work involves two factors: force and movement. Force is measured in pounds and distance. Therefore, work is measured in units called foot-pounds.

Friction is resistance that one surface creates during movement over another surface. The amount of friction depends upon the nature of the two surfaces and the amount of force pitting them together.

In many instances, friction can be helpful. For example, friction holds a box from sliding down an inclined ramp. The sand you throw on the sidewalk on an icy day increases the friction beneath pedestrians' feet. Nails hold wood together because of the friction between the nails and the lumber.

Friction is at work when an object in motion is slowed, when traction is acquired, and when motion from gravity is inhibited from overcoming an object. When a machine runs at high efficiency, friction is eliminated to the highest degree possible by oiling bearings and smoothing rubbing surfaces.

Friction occurs every time two surfaces move against one another. The work used in overcoming the frictional resistance does not appear in the work output. Therefore, more work is required to operate a machine inhibited by excess friction. Theoretically, no machine is 100 percent efficient. The efficiency of any machine is found by dividing the work output by work input.

Power & Horsepower

Power is the rate at which work is done. Horsepower is the unit of measurement by which power equivalent to 33,000 foot-pounds of work per minute (550 foot-pounds per second).

Force

Force is the pull of gravity exerted on an object or an object's thrust against friction. Force is applied to a machine; the machine, in turn, transmits a force to the load.

Measuring Force

Weight is a measurement of force on an object. Weight is measured using a scale. Scales are of two types: spring and balanced.

Gravity

Gravitation is a natural phenomenon by which all physical bodies are attracted to each other. Gravity is one of the fundamental laws of the physical universe. The Earth's gravity gives weight to physical objects and causes them to fall toward the ground when dropped. It is an important concept that must be understood to respond to many mechanical aptitude questions.

While a full discussion of gravity is beyond the scope of this guide, for the purpose of answering mechanical aptitude questions, be mindful of the following key facts:

- Gravity is the constant downward force that keeps people and objects on the Earth.
- The force of gravity creates resistance against the elevation of an object above a resting point.
- In general, the force of gravity exerted upon every object is the same, regardless of the object's weight, size, and shape. Thus, objects moving only by the force of gravity (i.e. free fall) will move at the same rate toward a resting point.

Pressure

Pressure is the amount of force contained within a specific area. All fluids (both liquids and gases) exert pressure. A fluid at rest exerts equal pressure in all directions. Three different gauges indicate the pressure of fluids: Bourdon gauge, Schrader gauge, and diaphragm gauge.

Bourdon Gauge

The Bourdon gauge works on the same principle as a paper party whistle, which straightens when you blow into it. Within the Bourdon gauge is a thin-walled metal tube flattened and bent into the form of a C. Attached to its free end is a lever system that magnifies any motion of the free end of the tube. As pressure increases, it travels through the tube. Like the snakelike paper whistle, the metal tube begins to straighten as the pressure increases inside of it. As the tube straightens, the pointer moves around a dial indicating the pressure in psi.

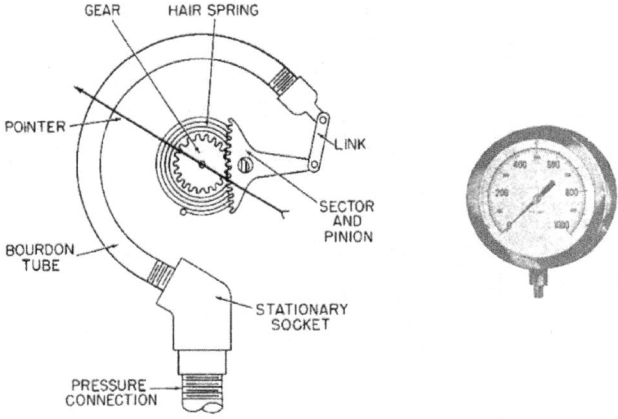

Diaphragm Gauge

The diaphragm gauge gives sensitive and reliable indications of small pressure differences. The diaphragm gauge measures the air pressure in the space between inner and outer boiler casings. In this type of gauge, a diaphragm connects to a pointer through a metal spring and a simple linkage system. One side of the diaphragm is exposed to the pressure being measured, while the other side is exposed to the pressure of the atmosphere.

Any increase in the pressure line moves the diaphragm upward against the spring, moving the pointer to a higher reading. When the pressure decreases, the spring moves the diaphragm downward, rotating the pointer to a lower reading. Thus, the position of the pointer is balanced between the pressure pushing the diaphragm upward and the spring action pushing down. When the gauge reads 0, the pressure in the line is equal to the outside air pressure.

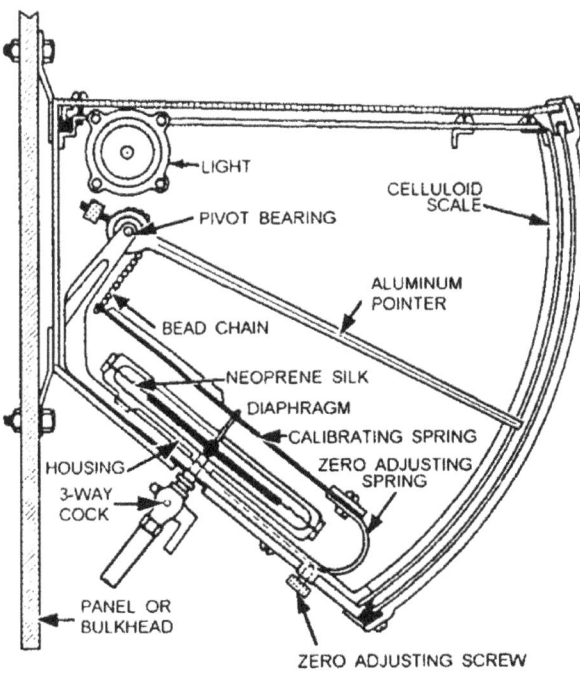

Schrader Gauge

In the Schrader gauge, liquid pressure actuates a piston. The pressure moves up a cylinder against the resistance of a spring, carrying a bar or indicator with it over a calibrated scale. The operation of this gauge eliminates the need for cams, gears, levers, and bearings.

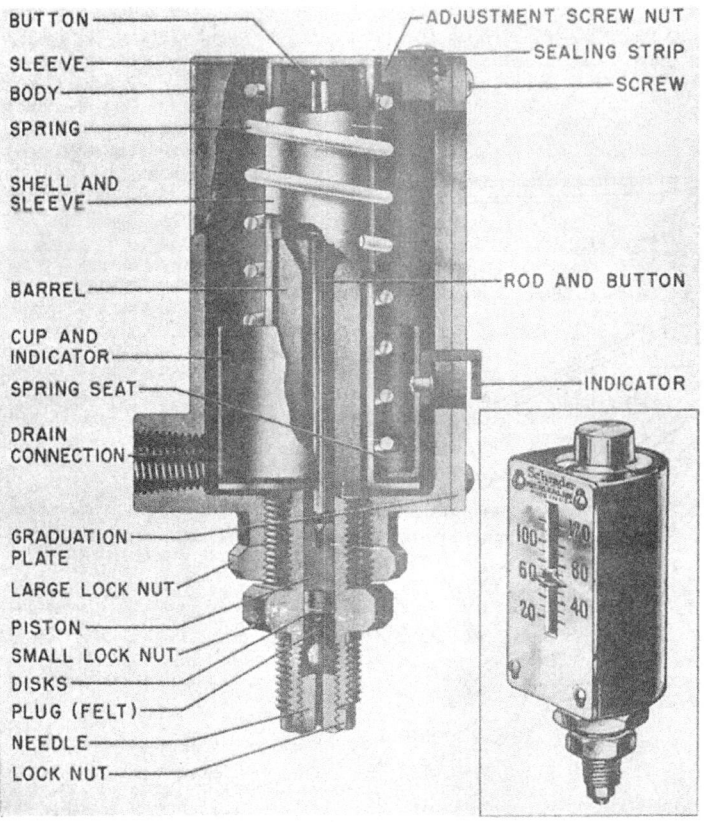

Questions:

1. When a chain hoist is used to multiply the force being exerted on a load, the chain is pulled at a faster rate than the load travels.

A. True

B. False

2. What are the six basic simple machines?

A. lever, block and tackle, inclined plane, engine, wheel and axle, and the gear

B. lever, block and tackle, wheel and axle, screw, the gear, and the eccentric

C. lever, wedge, wheel and axle, inclined plane, screw, and the pulley.

D. lever, inclined plane, gear, screw, fulcrum, and the torque

3. Which of the following simple machines works on the same principle as the inclined plane?

A. screw

B. gear

C. wheel and axle

D. block and tackle

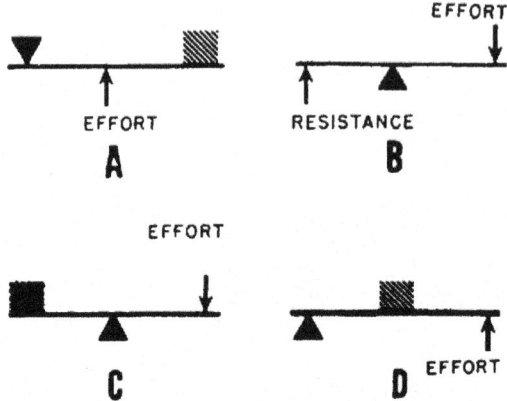

4. Which, if any, of the following parts illustrates a first-class lever?

A. C

B. B or C

C. D

D. none of the above

5. Which part illustrates a second-class lever?

A. B

B. C

C. D

D. A

6. What part illustrates a third-class lever?

1. A

2. B

3. C

4. D

7. Which of the following classes of levers should you use to lift a large weight by exerting the least effort?

A. First class

B. Second class

C. First or second class

D. Third class

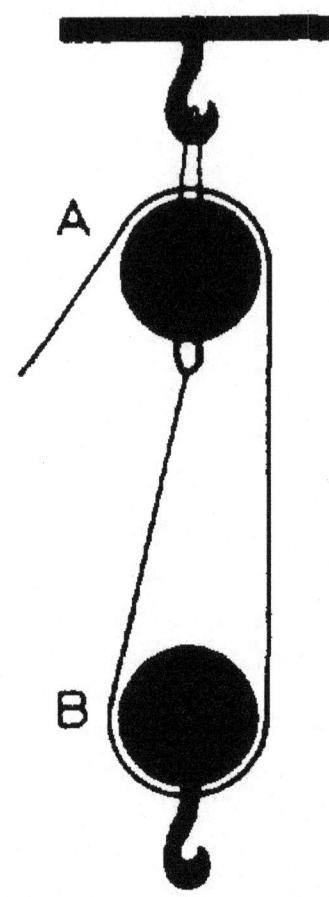

8. In the arrangement above, the purpose of block A is to

A. increase the mechanical advantage of the block

B. change the direction of the applied force

C. hold up block B

D. act as a runner for block B

9. The mechanical advantage of a wheel and axle depends upon the…

A. length of the axle

B. size of the wheel and the amount of the resistance

C. ratio of the radius of the wheel to which force is applied to the radius of the axle on which it turns

D. amount of force applied and the size of the wheel

10. The moment resulting from a force acting on a wheel and axle is equal to the…

A. amount of force required to produce equilibrium in a wheel and axle

B. ratio of the force to the distance from the center of rotation

C. distance from the point where the force is applied to the center of the axle

D. product of the amount of the force and the distance of the force from the center of rotation

11. What kind of wrench could you use that measures directly the amount of force you are exerting on the nut?

A. pipe wrench

B. torque wrench

C. spanner wrench

D. adjustable end wrench

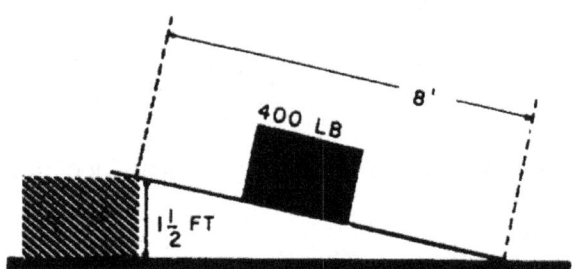

12. The theoretical mechanical advantage of the inclined plane is:

A. 3/16

B. 3

C. 5 1/3

D. 6

13. Neglecting friction, the force, needed to pull the crate up the inclined plane is:

A. 50 lb.

B. 75 lb.

C. 124 lb.

D. 600 lb.

14. Gears serve all the following purposes EXCEPT:

A. eliminating frictional losses

B. changing the direction of motion

C. increasing or decreasing the applied force

D. increasing or decreasing the speed of the applied motion

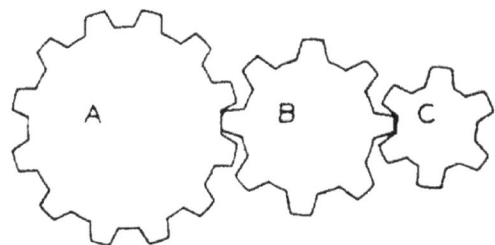

15. If gear A is rotated clockwise, what direction will gear C rotate?

A. clockwise

B. counterclockwise

16. If gear B is rotated counter clockwise, what direction will gear A rotate?

A. counterclockwise

B. clockwise

17. If gear C is rotated clockwise, what direction will gear A rotate?

A. clockwise

B. counterclockwise

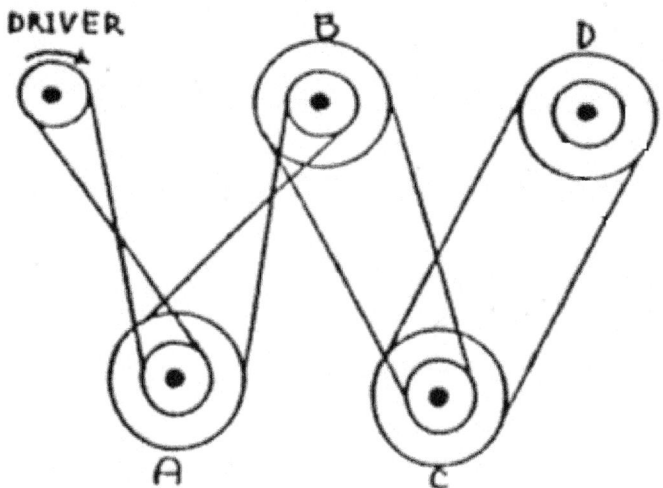

18. What direction is pulley D rotating?

A. clockwise

B. counterclockwise

19. What direction is pulley B rotating?

A. the same direction as A

B. the opposite direction as D

C. the opposite direction as A

D. Both A and C

Mechanical Ability Answer Key

1. A
2. C
3. A
4. B
5. C
6. A
7. A
8. A
9. C
10. D
11. B
12. D
13. B
14. A
15. A
16. B
17. A
18. A
19. C

Mechanical Ability, Visualization

Questions regarding visual/spatial relations usually require the identification of objects by pattern, shape, and/or spatial orientation. Often, several characteristics of an object are manipulated at the same time. Therefore, more than one characteristic of the referenced object must be considered to answer the question. This section will present typical visual and spatial relations questions including: hidden figures, spatial views, block counting, and paper folding questions.

This type of question requires forming mental images of what objects look like after they have been changed in some way. For example, a question may show a shape, and the candidate will be tasked with determining how the shape would look if it was flipped or rotated.

Key Points:

- Spot the target figure immediately and verify the choice by comparing it to the selection key (e.g. line length, symmetry, and angles).

- If unable to identify the target figure immediately, eliminate those choices that fail to match the key characteristics of the target (i.e. line length, symmetry, and angles) and evaluate the remaining choices again.

- Examine the configuration of blocks to determine where empty spaces are and where support is necessary to hold any block up (i.e. gravity).

- Assume patterns continue when blocks are hidden from view, unless there is evidence to indicate that the pattern does not continue.

- Make a record of known information before making inferences about less obvious parts of the problem.

Tips for Answering Visualization Questions:

- Mentally assemble the image before reviewing the available options.
- Attempt to match the available options to the mental image.
- If the mental image is not one of the available options, identify a unique characteristic (e.g. shape) of known information and try to locate that same characteristic in the answer choices.
- Study the cutout to identify any patterns. Start by finding a starting point, such as the top or front of the cutout, and noting what is adjacent to or opposite that point.
- Label parts of the cutout to help identify segments of the object.
- Look at the available options to eliminate choices that do not follow the observed pattern.
- If unable to eliminate all but one option, choose a different starting point and repeat the process until a solution is reached.

Visualization Practice Question Set:

1.

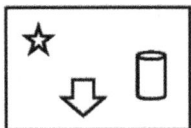

Which one of the images below represents the above image rotated clockwise 90 degrees?

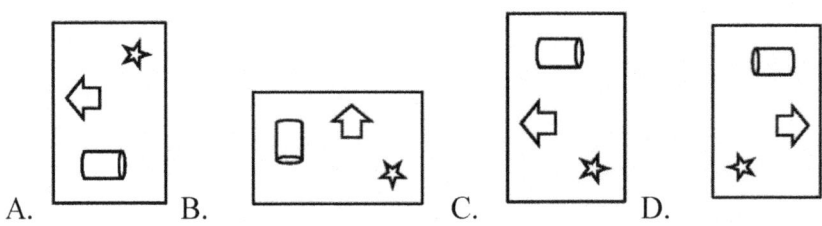

2.

Which one of the images below represents the above image flipped horizontally?

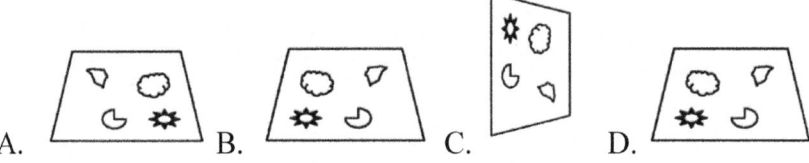

3.

Which one of the images below represents the above image flipped vertically?

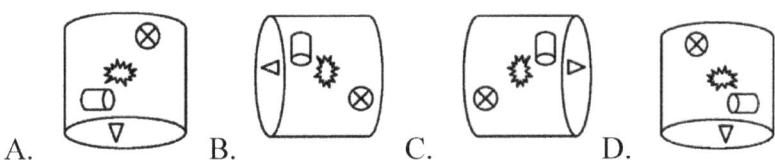

A.   B.   C.   D.

4.

Which one of the images below represents the above image rotated 90 degrees clockwise and then flipped horizontally?

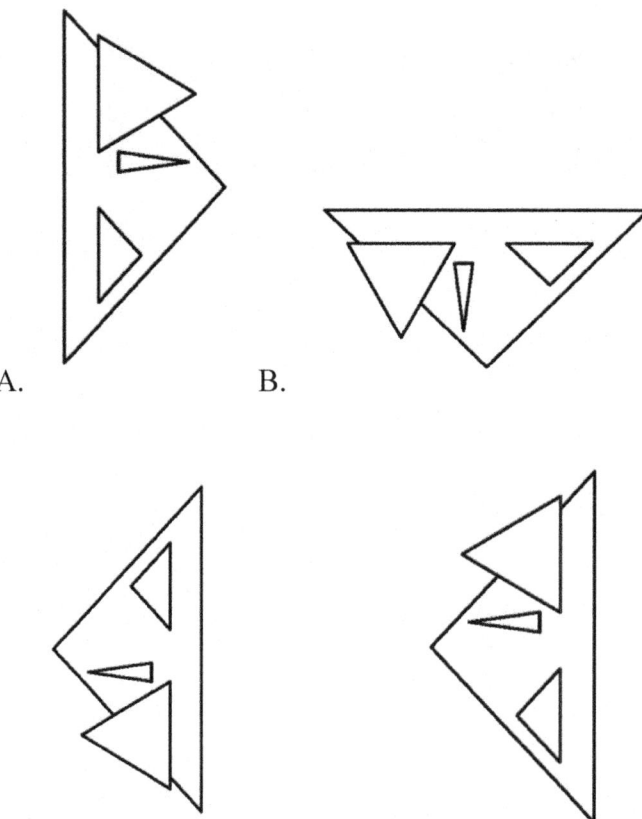

A.   B.

C.   D.

5.

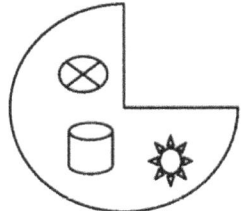

Which image represents the above image flipped horizontally?

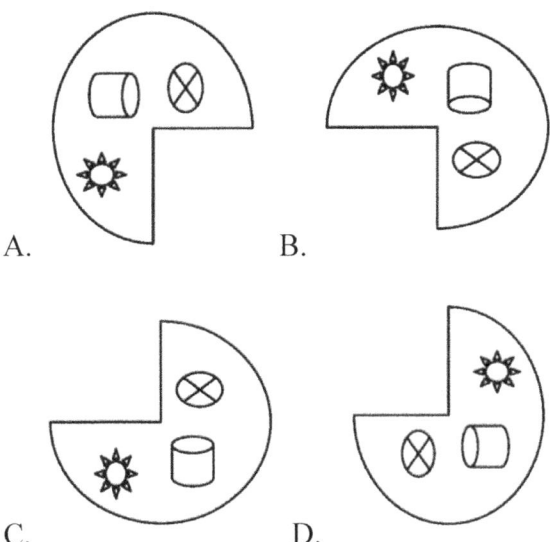

A.   B.

C.   D.

6.

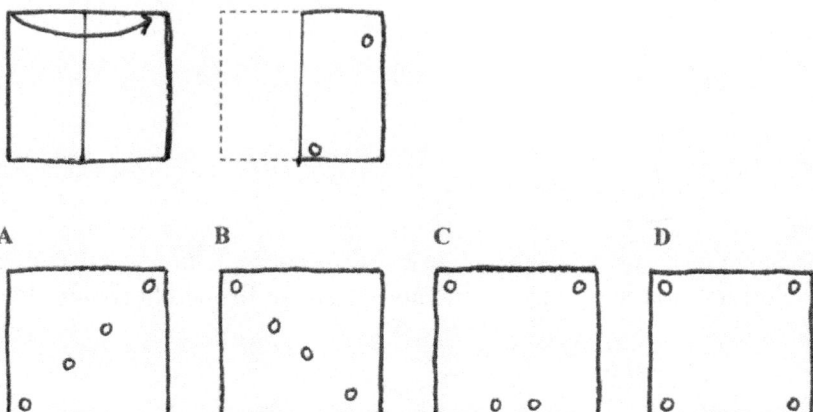

7.

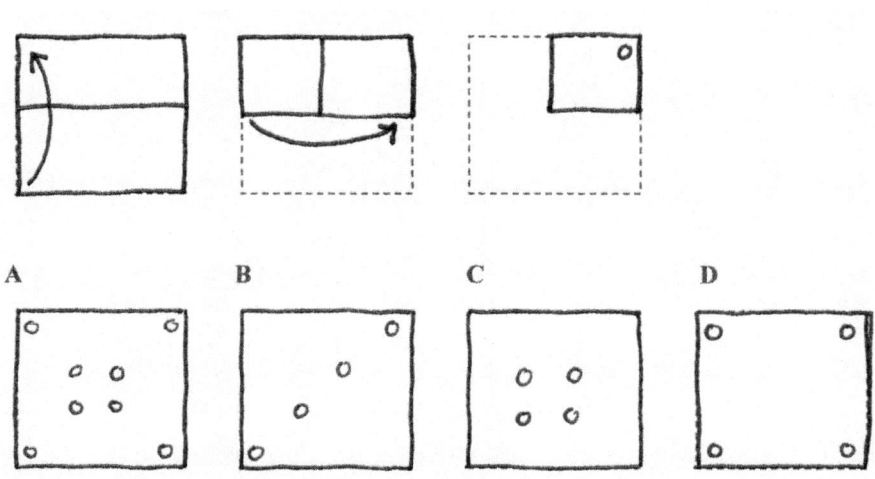

8.

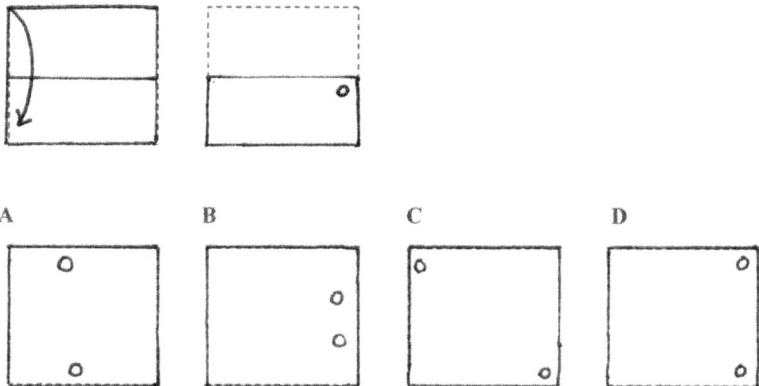

9.

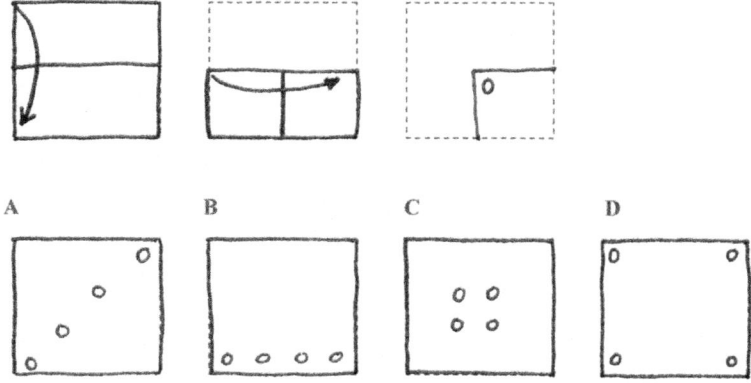

Visualization Answer Key:

1. A

2. A

3. A

4. D

5. C

6. C

7. D

8. C

9. C

Glossary

Accelerants. Materials, usually flammable liquids, used to initiate or increase the spread of fire.

Aerial ladder. A power-operated ladder permanently mounted on a piece of apparatus.

Apparatus. A fire truck.

Arson. The crime of willfully burning one's own or another's property.

Backdraft. The explosion of heated gases that occurs when oxygen is introduced into a space within a burning building where the oxygen has been depleted by the fire.

Basic life support. Noninvasive emergency life-saving care to treat airway obstruction, cardiac arrest or respiratory arrest.

Bunker coat, bunker pants. The protective coat and trousers worn by a firefighter for interior structural firefighting. Also called turnout coat and turnout pants.

Captain. The second ranking officer, between the lieutenant and battalion chief. Captains are often in charge of a company or fire station.

Carbon Dioxide. a colorless, odorless gas that is a normal product of combustion. In high concentrations, the gas can cause asphyxiation. It is also used in some fire extinguishers.

Carbon monoxide. A toxic gas, odorless and colorless, that produced when substances are incompletely burned.

Combustible. Capable of reacting with oxygen and burning if ignited.

Conduction. Heat transfer within an item or from one to another by direct contact.

Convection. Heat transfer by circulation within a gas or liquid.

Decontamination. "Decon" refers to the decontamination of equipment and personnel from bodily fluids or contaminates. It may also refer to "Haz-Mat" operations in the case of chemical spills or terrorist attacks.

Egress. A way out or exit.

Emergency medical technician (EMT). A professional who provides prehospital care for people who are sick or injured, including transport, medication and the use of defibrillators. EMTs have differing levels of training:

EMT -Basic. An emergency medical technician trained in basic emergency care skills, including oxygen therapy, bleeding control, cardiopulmonary resuscitation, automated external defibrillation, use of basic airway devices, and assisting patients with certain medication. Most EMTs fall into this category.

EMT – Paramedic. An emergency medical technician with the most advanced training, capable of cardiac monitoring, administering drugs, inserting advanced airways, manual defibrillation, and other advanced assessment and treatment skills.

Engine company. A group of firefighters responsible for securing a water source, deploying hose lines, conducting search-and-rescue operations, and putting water on the fire.

Engine. A fire truck capable of forcing out at least 750 gallons of water per minute, with a hose at least 1,000 feet long, and a water tank holding at least 300 gallons.

Fast Truck. FAST stands for Firefighter Assist and Search team. While usually a truck company at times engines and other units can be FAST. A FAST truck at a box stands by in case a firefighter becomes trapped, injured, etc.; they are tasked, along with the Rescue and Squad, with locating lost firefighters and removing them safely.

Fire code. A set of legally adopted rules and regulations designed to prevent fires and protect lives and property.

Fire hook. A tool to pull down burning structures; used in Colonial times as the only way to stop a fire.

First responder. The first trained person to arrive at the scene of an emergency to provide initial medical assistance.

Flameover (rollover). The rapid spread of flame over surfaces.

Flammable. Capable of being readily ignited.

Flashover. The stage of fire when all surfaces and objects are heated to their ignition temperature (flash point) and flame breaks out almost at once over the entire surface.

Flash point. The lowest temperature at which a liquid or solid releases enough vapor to ignite when mixed with air.

Halligan Tool- A tool used for forced entry.

Head of the fire. The main or running edge of a fire, the part of the fire that spreads fastest.

Hurst Tool- A hydraulic ram used for extrication and rescue work.

Ignition point. The minimum temperature at which a substance will burn.

Ignition temperature. The minimum temperature at which a fuel, when heated, will ignite in air and continue to burn; the minimum temperature required to for a self-sustained combustion.

Incendiary fire. An intentionally set fire.

Irons. The combination of an axe and Halligan tool used for forcible entry.

Lieutenant. A company officer who is usually responsible for a single fire company on a single shift; the first in line of company officers, in command when the captain is absent.

Life safety rope. Rope used solely for supporting people during firefighting, rescue, other emergency operations and training.

Line. One or more lengths of connected hose.

Mayday. Code that indicates a firefighter is lost, missing or requires immediate assistance.

Oxidation. A chemical reaction in which an element combines with oxygen. All fires are a form of oxidation.

PASS. Personal alert safety system. Device worn by a firefighter that sounds an alarm if the firefighter is motionless for a period.

Paramedic. An emergency medical technician (EMT) with the highest level of level of training. Most EMTs are not paramedics, so the terms should not be used interchangeably. Paramedics are trained to do cardiac monitoring, administer drugs, insert advanced airways, perform manual defibrillation, and conduct other advanced assessments and treatments.

Positive pressure ventilation. The practice of forcing contaminated air out of burning building by placing a blower in the doorway and blowing the air through a ventilation hole cut in the roof.

PPE. Personal protective equipment. The helmet, hood, coat, gloves, self-contained breathing apparatus and boots worn by firefighters to protect against heat and water.

Products of combustion. Heat, smoke and toxic gases.

Probie- A probationary firefighter. A typical probationary period lasts two years.

Pyrolysis. The chemical decomposition of a compound into one or more other substances by heat alone; pyrolysis often precedes combustion.

Radiation. Heat transfer through electromagnetic waves, without objects or gases carrying it along. Radiated heat goes out in all directions, unnoticed until it strikes an object.

Respirator. A mask worn over the mouth and nose to filter smoke and fumes from the air.

Response time. The time a fire company takes to get to a fire and begin fire operations.

Self-contained breathing apparatus (SCBA). Respirator with independent air supply used by firefighters to enter toxic and otherwise dangerous atmospheres.

Staging area. A strategically located area where support personnel, vehicles, and other equipment can be held in an organized state of readiness for use during an emergency.

Taxpayer. A mixed commercial/ residential building with little or no fire stopping between subdivisions over the ceiling, common cellars or cocklofts that run the length of the building, etc.

Thermal column. A cylindrical area above a fire in which heated air and gases rise and travel upward. The magnitude and intensity of a fire can often be judged from the thermal column.

Thermal imaging device. An electronic device that detects differences in temperature based on infrared energy and then generates images based on that data. Commonly used in obscured environments to locate victims.

Turnout coat and pants. The protective coat and trousers worn by a firefighter for interior structural firefighting. Also called bunker coat and bunker pants.

Under control. The stage of a fire at which it has been partially extinguished and authorities are confident can be completely extinguished.

Utility rope. Type of rope used for securing objects, lifting equipment, or blocking access to a scene. It is not to be used to support people.

Made in the USA
Las Vegas, NV
05 April 2022